Catherine
of Siena's Way

THE WAY OF THE CHRISTIAN MYSTICS

GENERAL EDITOR

Noel Dermot O'Donoghue, ODC

Volume 4

Catherine
of Siena's Way

by

Mary Ann Fatula, OP

Michael Glazier
Wilmington, Delaware

About the Author

Mary Ann Fatula, O.P., is a Dominican of St. Mary of the Springs, Columbus, Ohio. She received her doctorate in systematic theology from The Catholic University of America in 1981 and is presently associate professor and chairperson of the theology department at Ohio Dominican College in Columbus. Her articles have appeared in *One in Christ, Spirituality Today, Review for Religious, Thomist,* and *Theology Digest.*

Acknowledgements

Except where Catherine's version is quoted, Scriptural citations are from the Revised Standard Version of the Bible, Catholic edition, copyright 1965, 1966, by the Division of Christian Education of the National Council of the Churches of Christ in the U.S.A., and are used by permission.

Special gratitude is expressed to Paulist Press, Mahwah, New Jersey for their generous permission to cite passages from the following works:

Catherine of Siena: The Dialogue, translated by Suzanne Noffke, O.P. From the Classics of Western Spirituality Series, copyright 1980 by the Missionary Society of St. Paul the Apostle in the state of New York.

The Prayers of Catherine of Siena, translated and edited by Suzanne Noffke, O.P. Copyright 1983 by Suzanne Noffke, O.P.

Thanks is due also to Medieval & Renaissance Texts & Studies, Binghamton, New York, for permission to quote from the forthcoming *The Letters of Catherine of Siena,* edited and translated by Suzanne Noffke.

First published in 1987 by Michael Glazier, Inc. 1935 West Fourth Street, Wilmington, Delaware, 19805. © 1987 by Michael Glazier, Inc. All rights reserved.

   Library of Congress Card Catalog Number: 86-45350

   International Standard Book Number: 0-89453-589-7

Cover design by Brother Placid, O.S.B. Printed in the United States of America.

For My Father and Mother
Michael Nicholas and Rita Hyzy Fatula
with Gratitude and Love

Table of Contents

6 The Blood of Jesus: Mercy for the Human Heart   118

7 The Two Wings of Love   135

8 Trusting in the Providence of God   153

Editor's Preface

Up to quite recently mystics were either misunderstood or simply not understood. But now we are coming to see that, in T.S. Eliot's words, the way of the mystics is "our only hope, or else despair." As the darkness deepens, and the lights go out, those ancient lights begin to appear and to show us the way forward. They are not only lights to guide us, but are each a human countenance in which we can recognise something of ourselves—each is a portrait for self-recognition.

Unfortunately, the great Christian mystics have been generally presented as models of perfection or monuments of orthodoxy—sometimes, too, as inhumanly joyless and ascetical. Yet they were, above all else, men and women of feeling, always vulnerable, at times perhaps insecure and uncertain of the way ahead. For all that, they all shine with a special divine likeness and a special human radiance.

Each of the following portraits tries to present a true likeness of its subject, a likeness that comes alive especially in the ordinary and the everyday. In each case the author has been asked to enliven scholarship with personal warmth, and to temper enthusiasm with accurate scholarship. Each portrait hopes to be in its own way a work of art, something carefully and lovingly fashioned out of genuine material.

The main focus nevertheless is on the way in which each mystic mediates the Christian Gospel, and so gives us a deeper, richer, clearer vision of the Christian mystery. This kind of exposition demands the reader's full and prayerful attention. Each book is the story of a pilgrimage, for the mystic, the writer and the reader.

Noel O'Donoghue

Introduction

Many people today treasure the gifts of life, and yet they seem also to thirst for a fulfillment more profound than the limited satisfaction that work, relationships, or material possessions provide. Fifteen hundred years ago, Augustine identified this human hunger as a mystical yearning, a thirst for God.[1] We may be tempted to regard Augustine's insight with a degree of disbelief, however, when we apply it to ourselves; visions, stigmata, ecstasy—surely these are the experiences which characterize the saints and by their absence mark our lives as non-mystical in contrast.

Yet nothing could be further from the truth. Contemporary theologians such as Karl Rahner and William Johnston have stressed the insight of Aquinas and John of the Cross that mysticism stands at the heart of the Spirit's gifts and baptismal heritage intended for each of us.[2] Rahner expresses this truth with particular boldness: "The Christian of the future will be a mystic or not exist at all."[3] If these words startle us, perhaps we have misunderstood the nature of

[1] *The Confessions* 1.1.

[2] See Karl Rahner, "The Spirituality of the Church of the Future," in *Concern for the Church,* Theological Investigations 20 (New York: Seabury Crossroad, 1981), pp. 143-153; William Johnston, *The Inner Eye of Love* (New York: Harper and Row, 1978).

[3] *Concern for the Church,* p. 149.

mysticism. Mystics themselves tell us that they encounter God first of all not in visions and revelations but in the depths of their own lives, in the fiber of their own experiences. The triune God's intimate presence and creative activity in every human life thus define all true mysticism.[4] Precisely because the saints illumine for us the mystical dimensions of our own lives, theologians such as Karl Rahner have stressed the indispensability of re-discovering the mystics.[5]

Thus this book on Catherine of Siena, part of the Michael Glazier series on *The Way of the Christian Mystics*. Rather than providing a comprehensive biography of Catherine—excellent ones already exist—this volume offers an introduction to Catherine as friend, sister, and guide in the journey of mysticism meant for each of us. We would be hard pressed, perhaps, to find a more charming and passionate, a more affectionate and captivating, a more contemporary and relevant companion for our journey than this fourteenth century Dominican woman who spent her life not in a monastery or hermitage but deeply enmeshed in the civil and ecclesiastical events of her day.

It may be difficult at first to imagine the sheer compelling force Catherine exerted on her contemporaries, a power so warm and passionately human that even friends and disciples far older than she clung to her presence and refused to call her anything but "Mama." Her Dominican confessor, biographer, and intimate friend, Raymond of Capua, was himself continually amazed at the "mysterious attraction which was part of her," the "charm of her manner," and the way in which her "ever radiant face" inevitably "drove out despondency" in anyone near her.[6] People who came to her fearful and troubled left full of joy and peace; feuding fami-

---

[4]Karl Rahner, *Opportunities for Faith: Elements of a Modern Spirituality* (New York: Seabury Crossroad, 1974), pp. 40-41.

[5]*Ibid.*, pp. 125-26.

[6]Raymond of Capua, *The Life of Catherine of Siena* 1.6; in *The Life of Catherine of Siena*, translated, introduced, and annotated by Conleth Kearns, O.P. (Wilmington: Michael Glazier, Inc., 1980), p. 56. Future references to this work will be given by the letter R followed by the number of the part and chapter, and page number in Kearns.

lies sought reconciliation with one another, and those in her presence experienced a joy and vitality that could be expressed only in the spontaneous inner cry, "It is good for us to be here."[7]

Yet it was not simply Catherine's natural attractiveness that drew others to her. Even Raymond's enthusiastic love for Catherine still allowed him to admit that "she had nothing out of the ordinary in the way of good looks."[8] Love, rather than physical beauty, made her radiant—a passionate love for God and for the people treasured by God. Catherine's uninhibited spontaneity in expressing this love embarrassed her friends who sometimes took offense at her display of emotion in prayer, at the cries of her heart and voice, at her body's freedom to praise God with prostrations and bows and uplifted hands and arms. Just as freely was she spontaneous in her affection for others, embracing those who came to her and addressing her letters, "My dearest," "My very beloved."

More than anything, however, the power and warmth of her words drew people to Catherine. After three years of living as a hermit in her small room she emerged as a woman with both the inclination and gift for speaking, and speak she did. Raymond gives a charming account of this most powerful of Catherine's assets: "Without the shadow of a doubt [she would] have kept on talking of God, without bite or sup, for a hundred days and a hundred nights at a time, if only she had listeners who could keep following what she said and share in the conversation." And since nothing so exhilarated her as talking of God with "appreciative listeners," the longer she spoke, the more lively and invigorated she became.[9]

Raymond confesses, however, that he himself was not always one of these appreciative listeners: "It often happened, as she spoke to me of God...that her flow of speech

7R 1.2, p. 28.
8R 1.7, p. 66.
9R 1.6, p. 57.

would keep running on and on...But immeasurably below her level as I was myself in matters spiritual, and weighed down by fleshly sluggishness, I would slip off imperceptibly into dreamland." Absorbed in her topic, Catherine would keep right on talking. Finally noticing Raymond asleep, she would make a sudden noise to awaken him, adding with exasperation, "I might as well be talking to the wall as to you about the things of God."[10]

Yet even Raymond's "sluggishness" could not prevent his recognizing Catherine's remarkable gift for preaching. Her "charism of utterance" burst forth in words that "burnt like a torch," and her eloquence so touched hearts that even those who came to "deride or belittle" her would inevitably "leave her presence in tears."[11] Because Catherine spoke with the fire of the Holy Spirit rather than with the "language of learning, "over and over again" crowds of a thousand and more would gather just to see and hear her.[12]

As attractive as her words and manner could be, Catherine could also refuse to employ complimentary language when it was undeserved. She characteristically addressed members of the clergy as "very reverend" or "very dear father;" but to three Italian cardinals who had repudiated Pope Urban VI she writes "without reverence" because they have given up their claim to reverence.[13] Catherine's temerity showed itself in correcting even popes. When she urges Gregory XI to choose peace instead of war, she stresses that rather than a proud desire to "teach" Gregory, "Truth itself" prompts her letter.[14] And after encouraging Urban VI to be "virile" in dealing with his own vices and gentle in dealing with those of others, she concludes: "If I have dared to write

---

[10]R 1.6, p. 58.

[11]R Prologue, p. 8.

[12]R Prologue, p. 6; R 2.7, p. 227.

[13]Letter 310 to three Italian cardinals. Future references to Catherine's letters will be given by the abbreviation *Let* with the number in the Tommaseo edition, and where pertinent, the Dupré Theseider number in parentheses.

[14]Let T 209 to Pope Gregory XI.

with boldness, it is because I am forced to do so by the divine goodness."[15]

Besides admonishing those whom she should have feared, the sheer strength of Catherine's will spent itself on other tasks as well. The reader cannot help smiling as Raymond recounts how she worked miracles. When her friend Fra Santi was dying, the imperious Catherine gained his healing with the words, "I command you in the name of our Lord Jesus Christ, not to die!"[16] In Pisa she issued this order to a sick man, "It is my will that you should be troubled by these forces no more."[17] And her beloved friend and secretary Stefano escaped death when Catherine spoke her will: "I command you, in virtue of holy obedience, to suffer this fever no longer."[18]

Inspired by the Holy Spirit, Catherine addressed God with the same audacity. Raymond relates how the power of her intercessory prayer obtained what seemed to be miraculous outcomes in situations of particular need. To gain a dying man's conversion, for example, she "wrestled" with God, arguing that while he did not deserve mercy, Jesus deserved to give it. "Was this why you came down into the Virgin's womb...just to take stock of our sins and to punish them?...Give me back my brother."[19] Raymond interpreted the man's conversion as living praise of the "inscrutable providence" which roused Catherine's "ardent heart to this pitch of boldness." "You allowed that man to remain hardened in his sins up to the very last, as if you cared nothing for him. But all along you had planned to take his soul into your care."[20] Because of her audacious intercession, another man, reputedly a murderer, changed into the "most peaceable and

---

[15]Let T 364 to Pope Urban VI.

[16]R 2.8, p. 239.

[17] R 2.8, p. 243.

[18] R 2.8, pp. 246-47.

[19] R2.7, pp. 213-14.

[20] R 2.7, p. 215.

kindliest of men,"[21] and two criminals on their way to execution turned their blasphemous shouts into cries of repentance and praise.[22]

Especially in his moments of amazement at Catherine's boldness, Raymond himself was more than keenly aware that her life "was to follow lines far different from those of other women" of her time. [23] Twice God called her to change her life radically in preparation for an increasingly public ministry. The Lord drew her forth from three years of solitude at the age of twenty-one to serve her brothers and sisters: "You are now to plunge boldly into public activity of every kind with but one thought in mind, the salvation of souls."[24] Again, when she was twenty-seven, the Lord summoned her to a "radical change" that would involve traveling throughout Italy and France, into the presence of civil rulers, Church leaders, and the pope himself: "I will lead you forth and will lead you back again and you will carry with you the honor of my name."[25]

Catherine's life was not one she would have mapped out at first for herself; in the midst of the Church, at the heart of the crises which tore away at its very core, she emerged as a voice of truth and of love crying out finally with her life. Her call was not one she initially planned, and yet it was everything she was made to be. No half-heartedness made its home in Catherine; she was not a woman who could measure out her life in teaspoons, leaving small investments of herself in many places but not all of herself in any one. As she herself said, she was to the core of her being, a "fire."[26]

But she was also a sea of paradoxes: at once iron-willed and vulnerable, passionate and gentle, volatile and tender,

[21] R 2.7, pp. 219, 222.

[22] R 2.7, pp. 217-18.

[23] R 1.12, p. 108.

[24] R 2.5, p. 159.

[25] R 2.6, pp. 204-05.

[26] Prayer 12; *The Prayers of Catherine of Siena,* edited by Suzanne Noffke, O.P. (New York: Paulist Press, 1983), p. 104.

self-willed and surrendered. Like the God she called "insane with love," she was herself more than a little mad with love. The depth and breadth of the freedom Catherine needed to fulfill God's will for her impelled her to live consecrated to God, but not in a convent; her vocation lured her to a life and ministry at the very heart of the world loved by God. Her interior life pushed her into engagement with the people and events of her world, while her impassioned involvement in the crises around her in turn fed and deepened her interior life. Catherine's mysticism became not only integrated with but also inseparable from her own human life lived radically and passionately in and for the world and the Church she loved.

We look at Catherine and see the boldness of her love, this young woman who in her late twenties and early thirties stood as a word of fire in the Church and in the political and social crises around her; and we see the meagerness of our own hearts and lives in contrast. Our doubts and temptations, our struggles and distractions, our pretenses and excuses and escapes: what could Catherine know of these? History and legend paint a portrait of her as the outspoken fourteenth century woman whose love for the Church inspired the papacy's return to Rome after a seventy-year residence in France. Hagiographers recount her first vision at the age of six, her consecration to the Lord when she was seven, her survival for some periods on the Eucharist as her nourishment; her power to heal the sick and to convert the most hardened of sinners.

These facts are not untrue; yet this unschooled woman who with Teresa of Avila was first to be named woman doctor of the Church would herself give an account of her life far different from the one characterized by these exceptional marks of favor and success. If Catherine were to tell her own story, it would surely be from her experience of Paul's words: "If I must boast, I will boast of the things that show my weakness...that the power of Christ may rest upon me" (2 Cor 11:30; 12:9). She lived her life in the midst of the same struggles and temptations we know, and even among those far more violent than most of us will ever experience. And her life and presence say to us: it is not in spite of these struggles but in them that the word of truth becomes a word of grace for us.

Catherine knows our human weakness by her own experience, but we, too, know something of her heart and fire by our own experience. In opening ourselves to her, we begin to discover a woman so warm in her understanding and so contemporary in her relevance that she evokes from us not merely respect and admiration from afar, but also the intimate response of love and communion known by friends. And as we find mirrored in her the meaning of our own deepest struggles and aspirations, we begin to recognize the same mystery that claimed her secretly at work within our own lives as well.

Like Catherine herself, her mystical way has the power to surprise and delight and touch us not only with its marvelous paradoxes but also with its amazingly contemporary relevance. We perhaps both expect and fear to find in this fourteenth century Dominican woman a mysticism as extraordinary and far removed from us as we might have imagined her to be; and instead we find a friend and sister as close to us as our own heart, a mysticism as near to us as our own life. The Church itself says something of extreme import for us in celebrating her as one of its doctors and greatest mystics, for Catherine's mystical teaching focuses not on detailed descriptions of extraordinary phenomena but on the flesh and blood experience of every-day human life.

Instead of concentrating even on methods and states of prayer, her mystical way directs our gaze to the infinite truth and mercy of the triune God who comes utterly near to us, and to the compassion of Jesus whose blood has power to transform our human life in its most concrete and radical need. It is true that Catherine's own "every-day" experience, so deeply intertwined with the civil and ecclesiastical crises of her day, was nothing less than extraordinary for a woman of her time. But it was, nevertheless, the real world with its beauty and peace, with its sickness and poverty and war and division, that engaged every fiber of her energy. Her mystical life, far from enjoying an existence unrelated to the events of the world around her, comprised the whole substance of the life she lived at the heart of these events.

Far from directing our attention to the private devotions of a woman holy but far removed from the real world in her experience and life setting, Catherine's mystical way centers us in the truth and power of the Gospel itself. And because of this, Catherine would be the first to say that mysticism, the transforming reality of the triune God's utter nearness to us, depends not on extraordinary phenomena, and still less on an "extraordinary life," but rather on the absolutely simple and powerful Gospel way to live our life.

The mystical themes which I develop in these pages focus, therefore, as Catherine herself does, not on detailed descriptions of states of prayer, but on the power of the triune God to set our human life free for love and ministry to the Church and world. Her mystical way, especially relevant for us today, thus entails growing in Gospel attitudes of mind and heart open to experience God's closeness, not in withdrawal from the world God loves, but in passionate engagement with it.

Rather than following the logical and orderly sequence of a systematic presentation, Catherine's own style expresses the rich and passionate outpourings of a mind and heart whose themes, like the threads of a rich tapestry, continually and inextricably intertwine. I have tried, however, to reflect on her insights in a way that unfolds a certain order and progression in themes. To do so, I have used the original sources: her letters, prayers and *Dialogue,* as well as the biography of her written by her confessor, Raymond of Capua.

The following pages thus unfold Catherine's mystical way as it expresses the Gospel's power to transform how we live, in truth and in love, with surrender and with passion. After an overview of her life (ch 1), the book reflects on the following of Catherine's central mystical themes: We enter into the very meaning of our life by embracing God's will (ch 2) and by living the truth that sets us free (ch 3). The demands of an active life in turn lead us to intimacy with God in the "inner dwelling" (ch 4) in which we learn to pray (ch 5). Here, too, we discover the sacraments' power to bathe us in the mercy bestowed by the blood of Jesus (ch 6). This mercy draws us out of ourselves to a love that befriends our brothers and sisters (ch 7) and embraces a radical trust in God's providence (ch 8). Living the truth in love, we thus find the heart of mystical union, intimacy with the triune God (ch 9). God's selfless love in turn calls us to pour out our life in the Church for the world's salvation (ch 10). The mystical themes of Catherine which unfold in these pages thus reflect on the triune God's intimate presence and power to transform not only the way we pray but also and most deeply the way we live, until our life itself becomes a living prayer.

I wish to express here my deep gratitude to the many people whose prayer and assistance have helped me in the completion of this book: to my Dominican community, family, and friends for their constant prayer and encouragement; to Francis Gabriel Mahoney, O.P., Mary McCaffrey, O.P., Mary Michael Spangler, O.P., and Ennio and Rita Fatula Mastroianni for their very helpful suggestions; to my Dominican congregation of St. Mary of the Springs and Ohio Dominican College for moral support and financial aid in this project; to Rosalie Graham, O.P., librarian of Ohio Dominican College, and Kathleen Krick for her generous assistance; to Daniel F.X. Meenan, S.J., editor of *Review for Religious,* for permission to use articles previously published in this journal as the basis for chapters seven and eight; to Suzanne Noffke, O.P., for her inspiration and invaluable help; and to Michael Glazier for his light-hearted trust in God and in his authors.

May these pages entice the reader to seek out the original sources with fresh understanding and to discover in them the full treasure of Catherine's insight. And may Catherine herself inspire us to yield ourselves unreservedly to the triune God whose passionate love so completely claimed her.

1

Catherine in Context

The World of Catherine

Catherine's story, so intertwined with the ecclesiastical and civil events of her day, awakens us to an epoch not only fascinating but also remarkably contemporary in its resonance. Her lifetime, 1347-1380, spans a critical turning point in the Church's history. The ideal of a Europe united under one emperor and pope began receding before the reality of independent states warring for supremacy, and an already beleaguered Church faced further decline as often unworthy members repopulated the priesthood and religious orders after the Plague's devastating toll in 1348.

A world breaking away from its medieval framework had earlier witnessed the struggle of King Philip of France and Pope Boniface VIII in a power play that would have far-reaching implications for the pre-Reformation Church. In response to papal attempts to secure absolute authority over both Church and state, Philip forbade the contribution to Rome of money associated with French bishoprics. Boniface excommunicated Philip who retaliated by unleashing his henchmen on the pope; Boniface died several months later. Elected as Pope Clement V in 1305, Frenchman Bertrand de

Got remained in France, thus establishing a precedent for the choice succeeding popes would make for the next seventy years.

From their residence in Avignon, popes continued their rule in Italian lands through French delegates. Tuscany, Catherine's birthplace in the central section of Italy, especially balked at this foreign influence. At the same time, Florence, noted for its commerce and culture, grew impatient to assume what it saw as its rightful ascendancy over the other Italian states. Through continual feuds and bloody revolutions the people of both Florence and Siena won for themselves a representative government, and toward the last part of the thirteenth century a group of nine elected representatives—and later, a group of twelve—governed Siena. In both Florence and Siena, commoners and nobility alike coveted the privilege of the *popolani*—those eligible to rule.

Giacomo Benincasa of Siena counted himself among these *popolani*. A dyer of comfortable means, he married Lapa Piacenti, daughter of a poet and a quilt maker. Giacomo's generous and calm nature tempered Lapa's talkative and explosive disposition and brought some influence of serenity into the busy household.[1] Catherine, the twenty-fourth of their twenty-five children, was born in 1347, possibly on March 25; her twin sister Giovanna died soon after birth. Catherine quickly secured her own place in the large Benincasa family through her stubbornness, lively chatter, and disarming directness. These same qualities, purified and transformed, would later make their impact in a much wider arena; for Catherine Benincasa would be caught up into an extraordinary movement of the Spirit that would place her in increasingly expanding civil and ecclesiastical circles until she would find herself at the very heart of the ills not only of Italy and Europe but also of the universal Church itself.

[1]R 1.1, pp. 23-25.

A Dominican Call

Playful and ardent, Catherine was attracted even as a child to the services at the Dominican church near her home. The God she gradually came to know in these and in family settings became increasingly real to her, and when she was scarcely seven, she resolved in her child's way to consecrate herself to Jesus. This early religious intuition emerged with greater clarity and force several years later. At Catherine's entry into adolescence, Sienese custom severely curtailed her free-spirited play in the streets of Siena. Determined to arrange a financially profitable match for her daughter, Lapa encouraged Catherine's married sister Bonaventura to take the young girl under her tutelage.

With Bonaventura's help, Catherine learned how to use make-up and to dye her chestnut hair the blond color admired by Sienese men; in the excitement of this adult world, her earlier resolution not to marry seemed forgotten. But in 1362 Bonaventura died in childbirth. The death of her closest friend and confidante made an irrevocable impact on Catherine. Her grief at life's deceptions grew into a renewed choice of her childhood intuition: she would give herself to the Lord whom death could not take from her.[2]

The fifteen-year-old's ingenuity and will power had to face the immediate challenge of prevailing over Lapa's plans for her marriage. For support and advice in this venture, Catherine turned to her cousin and first confessor, Tommaso dalla Fonte. Orphaned by the plague in 1348, the young Dominican had been raised in the Benincasa home and Catherine trusted him.[3] Tommaso suggested that she offset marriage plans by cutting off her hair. When Catherine did precisely this, her horrified family undertook a concerted compaign to bring her to her senses. In an attempt to face Catherine with

[2]R 1.4, pp. 40-44.

[3]Tommaso dalla Fonte was related perhaps to the husband of Catherine's sister, Niccoluccia; her husband's name was Palmerio di Nese dalle Fonti [Arrigo Levasti, *My Servant, Catherine* (Westminster, Md.: Newman Press, 1954), p. 15].

the unenviable lot of women who refused to head house-
holds of their own, they made her responsible for the maid's
chores. But Catherine seemed not to mind; her still lively and
cheerful disposition soon won her father over, so that he
allowed her to live at home with no prospect of marriage.[4]

Yet Catherine still needed a way to secure her freedom to
live consecrated to the Lord outside the context of either
marriage or the convent. She was familiar with the *mantellate,* widows dressed in the Dominican habit who lived in
their own homes and devoted themselves to prayer and service of the poor and sick. Catherine resolved to join these
Dominican women, but because of her youth, neither Lapa
nor the *mantellate* themselves would hear of it.[5] Her strong
will won out over their objections, however, and by the age
of eighteen she was clothed in the Dominican habit.[6]

Catherine now began to live as a recluse, devoting her day
to prayer, and leaving the house only for daily Mass at San
Domenico, the church of the Dominican friars in Siena.[7]
This early period of withdrawal left varying impacts on
Catherine: although she learned to read in this time of solitude, the excessive penances she practiced permanently
damaged her ability to eat or digest food.[8] Most signifi-

[4]R 1.4, pp. 44-46; 50-52.

[5]According to Raymond, the *mantellate,* so named because of their black mantle
over the white Dominican habit, traced their origins to the time of Dominic in the
thirteenth century. Dominic enlisted the help of laymen to restore Church property
usurped by the state, and asked their wives to cooperate with their husbands'
undertakings. These men, originally called the *Militia of Jesus Christ,* later changed
their name to *The Brothers of Penance of Saint Dominic.* As their husbands died,
the widows remained faithful to the devotion which they had lived with their
spouses. Other widows began to associate themselves with these *Sisters of Penance
of Saint Dominic* and the movement spread throughout Italy. The widows eventually asked the Dominican priests to provide a rule and way of life for them even as
they lived in their own homes (R 1.8, pp. 70-73). Catherine was "the first and the
best in her city to receive the habit as a virgin; since her time many other virgins
there have followed in her footsteps" (R 1.7, p. 68).

[6]R 1.7, pp. 63-68.

[7]R 1.9, p. 76.

[8]Raymond notes that Catherine was absolutely unable to tolerate food; if she was
forced to eat, she suffered intense pain and "what had been violently forced down
was violently forced back again" (R 2.5, p. 161). Because of her critics, she did try to

cantly, however, the silence brought her face to face with the self she had not known, the part of her which desired ease and comfort rather than penance and dedication to God. In the midst of relentless temptations Catherine begged for a pure heart,[9] and the Lord answered her prayer by binding her to himself in the union of faith which Hos 2:19-20 promises: "I will betroth you to me in faithfulness."[10]

Ministering to Christ in the Poor

Catherine's life turned suddenly upside down. She had convinced herself earlier that God could claim her only if she cut herself off from the world; and yet, in spite of this, she could not escape the inner prompting to unite herself to the Lord by binding herself also to her brothers and sisters in need. In the solitude the Lord seared into her heart the truth that she could not love the unseen God if she did not love the brothers and sisters whom she could see (1 Jn 4:20).[11]

For three years, until 1370, the same undivided energy that she had given to solitude Catherine now devoted to caring for the Lord she found in the poor and sick. Siena knew the largesse of lay people dedicated to the poor by giving their wealth and lives to maintain hospitals, hospices, and foundling homes. As one of the *mantellate,* Catherine now entered wholeheartedly into this movement so obviously prompted by the Holy Spirit. She served those whom no one else would touch: the leprous and reviling

---

eat; but "nothing entered her stomach but it had to find its way back again by the same way; and if it did not do so, her whole body swelled up and suffered agonizing cramps....all this became a part of her daily routine up to the end of her life" (R 2.5, pp. 170,171). Her mother, Lapa, told Raymond that by the time Catherine was twenty-eight, her body mass had shrunk to half of what it had been when she was a robust young adolescent (R 1.6, p. 66).

[9] R 1.11, pp. 97-103.

[10] R 1.12, pp. 106-07.

[11] R 2.1, pp. 113-17.

Tecca; the abusive Palmerina; the dying Andrea, still strong enough in her cancerous illness to slander Catherine's reputation by accusing her of impurity.[12]

As she ministered to Andrea, Catherine would picture the wounded Christ in this poor woman. One day in order to overcome her revulsion for her, Catherine forced herself to drink of the putrid water in which she had washed Andrea's sores. But Catherine's disgust inexplicably turned to joy as the Lord gave her to drink mystically of his own life and blood; later, he invited her to give her heart to him in exchange for his own heart of unbounded love. Here, as it would happen again and again, Catherine's mystical experience of God followed upon her self-giving to the most needy of her brothers and sisters.[13]

Wherever she turned she saw Christ's face in the poor and suffering, and she felt impelled to give them not only her own clothes but also food, clothes, and items needed in the household. As a result, both Catherine and Giacomo suffered as family members upbraided his indulgence toward his daughter's prodigality. Yet Catherine could not do otherwise. Her solitude with the Lord at night pushed her out into the streets in the morning to minister to him in the poor and sick.[14]

Catherine's extraordinary love did not go unnoticed. In the midst of Siena's feuds and betrayals, she began to emerge unwittingly not only as a woman of love and peace, of passion and joy, but also as a woman of authority. Here was someone who knew and lived with God. People came to her home to talk with her, to spend time in the warmth and light of her presence, and a devoted *famiglia* of friends and disciples gradually grew up around her. In 1368 Tommaso dalla Fonte introduced to this circle of Catherine's the learned young Dominican, Bartolomeo Dominici. The group included also Catherine's sister-in-law, Lisa Colombini, and at

least two *mantellate:* Cecca Gori, mother of three Domini-
cans, and Alessa Saracini, the young aristocratic widow who
became Catherine's confidante and constant companion.[15]

Catherine's Growing Influence

The years of ministry to Siena's poor culminated in 1370
when Catherine became so gravely ill that those around her
thought she was surely dead. Catherine did recover, however, and the *famiglia's* inconsolable mourning turned to
ecstatic joy as they received Catherine back in good health.
But for Catherine, the experience heaped upon her its own
crushing weight, for as she later confided to her confessor,
Raymond of Capua, this "mystical death" exacted from her
a sacrifice of extreme cost. The Lord had answered her
desire to be with him in death by bringing her back to life.
Her vocation, it became clear, was to spend her life here in
claiming others for God.[16]

Catherine's place of ministry was no longer to be the hid-
denness of the home, nor even the streets of Siena, but the
arena of the entire Church. She was to care for the poor and
to preach the Word with a power that would resound
throughout the world. From 1370 until 1374, Siena witnessed countless conversions, as Catherine's word brought
hardened sinners and proud intellectuals alike to repentance.
The grace and power of her presence reconciled divided families and warring factions; in her company, notorious criminals wept openly for their crimes.

During this period the young Dominican, Simon of Cortona, and the poet, Neri di Landoccio Pagliaresi, joined her
group of disciples. With Neri as her secretary, Catherine
began to seek the conversions of people outside of Siena
through an extensive correspondence with lay people and
clergy, with prelates and civil rulers. When she traveled to

[15]R 3.1, pp. 314-18.
[16]R 2.6, pp. 186-88, 200-05.

Florence in 1374, persons of every rank sought her out; Nicolo Soderini, a city governor, was one among many in this city who formed a close and lasting friendship with Catherine.

Here, too, Catherine perhaps encountered for the first time the aristocratic and learned Dominican Raymond of Capua (Raimondo delle Vigne), who would become her confessor, biographer, and closest friend. The Dominican chapter held in Florence that year had assigned Raymond as lector in Sacred Scripture and director of studies at the Dominican house in Siena, and the Master General of the Order, Elias of Toulouse, apparently appointed Raymond also as Catherine's confessor.

In July of 1374, Catherine returned to a Siena ravaged again by the plague; from May until October priests and lay people alike fled the city as the disease spread uncontrolled. According to Simon of Cortona, the younger Dominican friars were so consumed with fear of infection that they refused to minister with the priests who chose not to flee.[17] But Catherine stayed and spent herself in caring for the victims. Inspired by her selflessness, other *mantellate* and Dominican friars, among them Raymond of Capua, ministered with her.

Seventeen years older than Catherine, Raymond had achieved a reputation of respect in papal and political circles. As he learned to know her, he became also her trusted friend, and through his influence Catherine increasingly assumed an important role in these same public circles. Two existing letters of Catherine written during 1374—when she was twenty-six—evidence her growing reputation among men of high political and ecclesiastical rank. One letter addresses Piero Gambacorta, a ruling lord of Pisa;[18] the second letter urges Cardinal Iacopo Orsini to press for Pope Gregory XI's fidelity to his promises of returning the papal

[17]Levasti, p. 133.
[18]Let T 149 (DT 22).

residence to Rome and of inaugurating a crusade to the Holy Land.[19]

Reports of Catherine's extraordinary love and courage in ministering during the plague had spread to other cities, and, inspired by what he had heard, Gambacorta invited her to Pisa. At first, Catherine declined his invitation, but as she saw that the ideals of peace and cooperation among the Italian states had won his commitment not simply for economic reasons but also for spiritual ones, she soon became convinced that God wanted her to go there. Accompanied by Raymond, Bartolomeo, and Tommaso, she departed for Pisa sometime after January 1375.

In this city noted for its past naval victories, Catherine's zeal for a crusade found new inspiration and she began preaching its cause with increased intensity. The time in Pisa also held significant personal growth for Catherine. On April 1, 1375, while in prayer after Holy Communion in the church of Santa Cristina, she felt the Lord grant her desire to share in his passion by giving her in an interior manner the pain of his own wounds—a pain which, she confessed later to Raymond, never left her.[20] From this time forward, Catherine's preaching assumed new intensity as the fire and warmth of her words touched and converted people of every rank.

Encouraged by Pisa's commitment of two galleys for the pope's safe return to Rome, Catherine began to preach with renewed energy the urgency of such a move. In Pisa, too, she learned of the English mercenary, John Hawkwood, whose company ravaged the Italian states unable or unwilling to pay him dues. The twenty-eight-year-old Catherine, at once naive and bold-spirited, wrote to Hawkwood exhorting him to direct his violent instincts instead toward heading a crusade to the Holy Land.[21]

Possibly in June of 1375, Catherine returned briefly to Siena, long enough to be present at the execution of a Peru-

[19]Let T 223.
[20]R 2.6, pp. 185-86.
[21]Let T 140 (DT 30).

gian noble, Niccolo di Tuldo. Condemned to death for inflammatory remarks against the Sienese government, the young man was so touched by Catherine's ministering to him that his change of heart seemed almost miraculous. Under her influence, blasphemy and rage at his condemnation gave way in him to desire for a martyrdom filled with love. Catherine kept her promise of staying with Niccolo until the end, and at his execution she received the young man's severed head into her hands. The experience was a deeply mystical one for Catherine and made a lasting impact on her. In light of her own thirst to give her life for the Church's reform, she interpreted Niccolo's death as the first fruits of those whose blood would be powerful in Christ's blood to win this renewal.[22]

Mediating Peace

In July of 1375, Catherine returned to Pisa where she heard that Pope Gregory had encouraged preaching of a crusade to the Holy Land. Fired by the thought of conversions to the Lord, Catherine entered into the preaching with vigor.[23] While she was at Pisa, Florence sent reports that the pope had refused needed supplies of corn to Florence and that he had engaged the military services of John Hawkwood. These rumors supplied Florence with the occasion to stir up support for a league aimed at economic independence from the French papacy.[24]

Urging other Italian states to stand with them, Bologna joined Florence and Milan in a Tuscan league against the pope on July 24; on August 14, a government of the Eight responsible for overseeing the war against the papacy took power in Florence. One by one, other Italian states supported the revolt. Heartsick at these developments, Cathe-

---

[22]Let T 273 (DT 31) to Raymond of Capua.

[23]R 2.10, pp. 266-69.

[24]R 2.10, p. 264.

rine undertook a passionate preaching crusade urging loyalty to the pope, and in September she traveled to nearby
Lucca to encourage this city's allegiance to Gregory XI.

At the end of 1375 Catherine returned to Siena to find
that her own city had joined the Tuscan league on November
27. An unexpected consolation, however, provided her some
relief in her distress. Not long after her return, Stefano
Maconi, a young nobleman of Catherine's age, had sought
her out as a mediator in a family feud with the Tolomei. The
peace and joy he found in her presence inspired him to join
her *famiglia,* and with Stefano serving as another devoted
secretary, Catherine began writing directly to the pope.
Convinced that she must awaken Gregory to the collapse of
the Church around him, she wrote urging him to make peace
with the Tuscan League and to return to Rome. She encouraged him also to inaugurate the crusade he had promised,
and to undertake a courageous reform of the Church
through the choice of holy prelates.[25]

On February 11, 1376 Gregory entered into an open test
of wills with Florence. The city's leaders who had been
summoned to appear in trial before him failed to prove their
avowed loyalty, and Gregory placed Florence under an
interdict. Celebration of the sacraments was forbidden in the
city, citizens were encouraged to seize the property of their
rebellious leaders, and any person offering economic or political support to Florence was excommunicated. Suddenly,
Italian states previously loyal to Florence defected.

Catherine was beside herself with grief at the developments, but on April 1, 1376, still perhaps in Siena, she began
to see the civil and ecclesiastical tragedy in a new light. In
prayer it seemed to her that Muslims and Christians alike
were entering into the wounded side of Christ and that she
herself was bearing the olive branch of peace to them.
Instead of signaling the Church's ruin, the war against the
papacy began to symbolize for her the mystery of the grain
falling into the ground to die, only to be reborn anew with

[25]R 2.10, pp. 266-68.

vigor and purity; through this tragedy the Church would finally be reformed.[26] Filled with joy and renewed courage, Catherine wrote a little while later to the leaders of the Guelphs in Florence, offering her services as a mediator in the task of reconciliation with the papacy. In the hope that Gregory would be all the more favorably inclined toward them because of her, the Guelphs accepted her proposal.[27]

Catherine and about twenty-two of her disciples arrived in Avignon on June 18, 1376. From that date until September, she met perhaps several times with the pope, urging him to deal gently with the Florentines and to keep his word by embarking for Rome. On September 13, Gregory fulfilled his promise and embarked on the first part of the journey to Rome. Soon afterward, Catherine and her group set out for Genoa, arriving in Siena at the end of 1376 or in early 1377.

In her home city Catherine turned her attention to a plan she had long cherished: to establish a convent of enclosed nuns for her disciples drawn to religious life. Nanni di Ser Vanni, a wealthy and sometimes ruthless man who had come under Catherine's influence during this time, offered her, at her request, his abandoned fortress at Belcaro near Siena.[28] While overseeing this foundation, Catherine traveled frequently throughout Italy in the spring of 1377, preaching with a power and warmth that attracted thousands of people from the countryside to hear her.[29]

In October of 1377 Catherine accepted Agnolino Salimbeni's invitation to Rocca de Tentennano at Val d'Orcia in order to mediate peace between him and his brother. But during her absence Sienese citizens accused her of plotting against them—a charge which cut at Catherine's heart since, as she later wrote, her only plot had been to gain conversions to the Lord. At Val d'Orcia she may also have learned to write, a gift she felt the Lord granted her as an outlet for her

[26]Let T 219 (DT 65) to Raymond of Capua.

[27]Let T 207 (DT 68) to the Signori of Florence.

[28]R 2.7, pp. 223-26.

[29]R 2.7, p. 227.

heart's outpourings after prayer. A letter which Catherine sent to Raymond in October, 1377 from this place contains an account of an experience in prayer which she would later use as an outline for her "book," the *Dialogue*.[30]

After Catherine's return to Siena in December, Gregory asked her to negotiate peace with the Florentines on his behalf. Catherine accepted, travelling to Florence probably in the spring of 1378. Her charm and holiness won her many friends in this city, among them the prominent Canigiani family. Especially dear to her was the young nobleman Barduccio Canigiani, who joined her company to serve as her trusted companion and secretary.

Upon her arrival in Florence, Catherine had first concentrated on urging the citizens to observe the interdict, but she soon unwittingly became caught up in more political intrigues. Victims of the Florentine practice of "admonishing," arbitrarily excluding certain people from office, stirred the lower class to riot. Members of the wealthy Guelph party, including the Soderini and Canigiani families, were among those who suffered the violent attack. Enemies accused Catherine of involvement in the plot and of inciting the riot through her alleged encouragement of unjust admonishing. In June of 1378, an angry mob bent on her death approached her in the garden of the home provided for her by Pietro Canigiani. Lisa, Neri, and Barduccio were with her. As the assassin drew near, Catherine's joy and courage at the thought of martyrdom disarmed him; he turned away, leaving her to weep at the dream that had slipped from her hands.[31]

On March 27, 1378 Gregory XI died and the newly elected archbishop of Bari, Bartolomeo Prignano, took the name Urban VI; bent on a rigid Church reform, the man soon emerged as a tyrant. On May 16, French cardinals withdrew in protest to Anagni, the Curia's summer home, and on August 9 proclaimed Urban's election invalid. Their justifi-

[30]Let T 272.
[31]R 3.6, pp. 385-86; Let T 295 to Raymond of Capua.

cation: that fear of the Roman mobs had forced them to choose an Italian. Gathered again at Fondi on September 20, the French cardinals elected the notoriously ruthless Cardinal Robert of Geneva, and on October 31, he was crowned as anti-pope Clement VII.

Called to Rome

On July 18, 1378 Florence had achieved with Urban VI a concordance in which Catherine finally had played no part; after nearly seven months in Florence, she quietly returned home[32] and there in Siena finished her "book" in October of 1378.[33] For some time Catherine had hoped to support Urban by her own presence in Rome, but the criticism of Sienese citizens and the gossip of some of the *mantellate* opposed to her frequent traveling augmented her own sense of uselessness in what had transpired at Florence. When Raymond sent word that Urban wanted her in Rome, she refused to depart without written evidence of the pope's request.

Raymond procured the necessary document from Urban and on November 23, 1378 Catherine arrived in Rome. Although the entire *famiglia* wanted to accompany her, in the end only twenty-four of her disciples—eight women and sixteen men—were able to journey with her. After a short stay in the house provided for them by Urban in Rione della Colonna, they rented a house in Via Santa Chiara. Here Sienese pilgrims lodged, and an endless stream of people from the area came to speak with Catherine. The women of the company took turns each week in caring for household needs; and, although the group existed only on alms, the number fed at their table often reached forty. When there was no food, Catherine herself would go into the streets to beg for bread.[34]

[32]R 3.1, p. 309.
[33]R 3.3, pp. 324-26.
[34]R 2.11, pp. 279-80.

In January of 1378, Raymond had been elected prior of the Dominican Church of the Minerva in Rome, and Catherine was overjoyed at the opportunity of being with him again. Raymond also was happy at the reunion, but he was even more pleased at the enthusiastic reception accorded Catherine when she accepted the pope's invitation to address him and a small number of cardinals still loyal to him. But Catherine's and Raymond's joy in each other's presence was short-lived, for in December Raymond had to leave on a papal mission to preach a crusade in France against Clement VII. Catherine never saw Raymond again. In January of 1379, when Raymond heard of plans to assassinate him, he turned back. Sympathetic toward Raymond's fear, Urban asked him to stay at Genoa to preach the crusade. Catherine was crushed; what she viewed as the cowardice of her trusted friend deepened the wounds she felt at being left in Rome without his support.

Several months later, Urban asked Raymond to resume attempts at winning over the French king to the Roman papacy. Hearing of further betrayals among the Spanish who were to have given him safe passage, Raymond made no attempt to go. The pope understood the impossibility of the situation. Catherine did not. "If you could not get there upright, you could have gone on all fours,...if you had no money you could have begged your way." Feeling herself responsible for her friend's cowardice in the face of what could have been a glorious martyrdom, Catherine writes, "Am I always, because of my faithlessness to shut the gates against Divine Providence?...Lord, unmake me and break my hardness of heart, that I not be a tool which spoils your works."[35]

The one who "spoils" God's work. The words betray the wound that began to devour Catherine, the crushing sense of her own responsibility for the Church's destruction. If she had not encouraged the pope's return to Rome, the schism would never have happened. She had labored with every

---

[35]Let T 344 to Raymond of Capua.

fiber of her being for the Church's reform, only to find herself defending as pope a hated tyrant. She had spent herself at Pisa and Lucca to prevent their rebellion against Urban and they had ignored her. Florence had made peace with Rome not only without her but also in mockery of her proffered help. "Any contemporary speculating on her political action would see all the threads of her life tangled and twisted into a most ignominious pattern of failure. Her work did not make sense."[36]

Her energies poured out in selfless love for those close to her did not make sense either. Unwittingly, Catherine's friends had abandoned her. Even as they loved and offered her their presence and support, some betrayed her and left her utterly alone. Raymond's cowardice had refused the martyrdom she bitterly longed to have as her own. The disciples she left behind in Siena as a close-knit family had disbanded within two months of her departure; a letter of Cristofano Guidini to Neri dated January 14, 1379 reads: "Tell our little mother that we are all fallen apart; she must give us some rule which, out of respect for her, we can obey, and which may gather us together in memory of her."[37] The energies she had poured out on her *famiglia* had come to nothing.

Her cherished dream for a "papal council" of holy men and women gathered in Rome to support the pope and to intercede for the Church's reform also failed miserably. Among those who refused to join her was her trusted friend William Flete. Catherine saw the "perfect completion of her own defeat. What she loved best in the world had failed her."[38]

Her sense of responsibility for the Church's ills became a weight which crushed her body as well as her spirit. Beginning on January 1, 1380 Catherine's health declined disas-

[36]Alice Curtayne, *Saint Catherine of Siena* (London: Sheed and Ward, 1932), p. 155.

[37]Levasti, p. 371.

[38]Curtayne, p. 178.

trously; her body seemed on fire with thirst. On January 29, against the backdrop of rumored uprisings against Urban, she suffered severe convulsions. For forty-eight hours Catherine battled what seemed to her to be demons mocking the meaning of her life.[39]

Aided by Barduccio, Catherine had made the mile-long journey to St. Peter's every morning for Lenten Mass. On the third Sunday of Lent she paused as usual to gaze at Giotto's mosaic on the inner facade of St. Peter's. Pictured was the disciples' small ship caught in a storm at sea. On this day the ship assumed dimensions of overwhelming reality and proportion for Catherine, as it became for her the Church about to be crushed by its division and sin. She felt the whole weight of the ship on her shoulders, yet she was powerless to prevent its shipwreck.

After this day, Catherine would not walk again. On Sexagesima Sunday, February 26, she felt the Lord take the "vessel" of her body and "refashion" it anew in self-giving for the Church.[40] On the dawn of Sunday, April 29, her companions heard Catherine struggle with what seemed again to be demonic forces attacking and mocking her. Earlier in the month Catherine's beloved friend, Stefano, had come from Siena; assured of her eventual recovery, he had left again. Lisa and Barduccio were there, but Raymond was not. At 9:00 a.m. that morning, held in the arms of Alessa, Catherine died. Her last words called out for the mercy of Jesus' blood upon her.[41]

---

[39]R 3.2, p. 320.

[40]Let T 373 to Raymond of Capua.

[41]R 3.2, pp. 320-23; R 3.4, pp. 334-41.

2

Embracing the Will of God

"Behold, I am the handmaid of the Lord; let it be to me according to your word" (Lk 1:38). With Mary and all those who have ever yielded themselves to God, Catherine learned to embrace God's will in her life not as an arbitrary decree demanding her compliance, but as the abyss of love which enfolded her in nothing but mercy. She discovered what those who love understand, that it is no easy thing to let go of our self-enclosed existence and to entrust ourselves to another. Yet Jesus' absolute union with his Father's will attracted Catherine to the same mystery which evoked Mary's unreserved response. As she thought of how God humbly waited at the "door" of Mary's will and would not enter without the consent of her love,[1] she came to realize that the Lord can fully possess only the one who freely opens

---

[1]Prayer 18; in Suzanne Noffke, O.P., ed., *The Prayers of Catherine of Siena* (New York: Paulist Press, 1983), p. 161. Future references to the prayers of Catherine will be cited by the number of the prayer and the page in Noffke's edition.

to him the "gate" of her freedom. She pictured Jesus as the sun knocking at the "shuttered window" of our will, flooding our being with the warmth and joy of his sunlight the very moment we open the shutters.[2] In this way she learned to see God's will as the abyss of love to which Jesus himself had surrendered his life and being, and into whose tender depths she too desired to plunge herself without reserve.

Entering into the Height and Depth of God's Will

What did it mean for Catherine to yield herself increasingly to the "tender will of God"? Her life evokes images of a woman utterly clear and confident about her meaning, surrendering herself from the start to an unequivocal call from God without resistance or hesitation. Yet her real story is one not only of clarity and openness, but also of initial reluctance and refusal, and of insecurity and fear and doubts that endured in some way to the end. The figure of Catherine resolutely correcting civil and church leaders gives way to that of a young woman on her death bed tempted to believe that her whole life had been a sham and illusion. Those who were with Catherine as she lay dying heard her struggle with doubts that plagued her: had her life been an embracing of God's will or her own?

Indeed, she could well question whether she had embraced unreservedly God's will. Ambiguity and failure enshrouded her in her own lifetime, and, like Jeremiah, she seemed seduced into a path that others could mock for its bitter deception. Her thirst to be one with God's will drove her to sacrifice her life and reputation. At a time when no respectable woman would appear in public unaccompanied, Catherine pursued with the independence of a man her work for the poor and her ministry of peacemaking. Because her devoted followers included unmarried men who served as her secretaries and constant companions, critics accused her

[2]Pr 15, p. 130.

of impurity and of lust for the accolades of fawning people.

Catherine's lifework met the same fate as her reputation. She poured out her energies for the papacy's return from Avignon to Rome for the sake of unity, and in the end witnessed a Church far more divided than before her efforts. At her death two papal claimants were vying for the loyalty of Europe, and afterwards the number would grow to three. Like her labors for ecclesiastical reform, her peacemaking missions among the warring Italian states made no enduring impact on the world. The *famiglia* gathered devotedly around her and on whose continued communion she counted for lasting fruit disintegrated soon after her death; the crusade she passionately advocated did not materialize. Not one of her life's great works achieved any final outcome except failure.

And yet in freely and wholeheartedly entering into what she called the "tender will of God," she accomplished God's plan of love for her far more wondrously than she could have imagined. Yielding her entire being to the Father's will as Jesus had done, she opened herself to the infinite flood tide of mercy that breaks apart narrow human plans and frees us for a life of inconceivable depth and breadth. Raymond's account of the path by which God drew Catherine to the full embrace of his will for her underscores the struggle which ended her early solitude and reawakened her childhood attraction, not to the eremitical life, but to apostolic preaching. She began to realize that her deepest inclination was not to isolation but to the communion and ministry at the heart of the Dominican call. In her sadness at abandoning solitude she felt the Lord invite her rather to rejoice in the breadth of the life for which she herself had longed since her childhood.[3]

Yet Catherine's initial response was to chide the Lord for foolishness in summoning her to preaching and peacemaking, ministries inaccessible to women of her day: "My very sex, as I need not tell you, puts many obstacles in the way.

---

[3] *R* 1.2, p. 116.

The world has no use for women in work such as that, and propriety forbids a woman to mix so freely in the company of men." In response to her objections, the Lord reminded Catherine that the divine wisdom has made the human race both male and female, and that the "tender will of God" has generous and amazing ways of accomplishing its plans. "Does it not depend on my own will where I shall pour out my grace? With me there is no longer male and female, nor lower and upper class; for all stand equal in my sight." Catherine, a woman, had been chosen for this public ministry precisely because God wished to humble the pride of men, "especially the pride of those who regard themselves as wise and learned men" and to put them "back in their place."[4]

Raymond stresses the import of God's call to Catherine for the men of the Church. Just as God sent unschooled apostles to confound the arrogance of both Jews and Gentiles, the Lord sends to church leaders "women filled with the power and wisdom of God." Those who treat these women "with disdain" will bear the weight of the divine "judgment;" for, instead of exalting them, their pride will reduce them "lower still." Yet if men listen humbly, "welcoming and heeding, with all due submission, the women" God sends them, the divine mercy will be outpoured in the Church.[5]

Catherine herself was to undertake boldly whatever task the Holy Spirit inspired in her, confident that God's closeness to her would not diminish but would deepen and guide her in everything.[6] As she began to yield herself to God's will, Catherine's life opened to a ministry of preaching and peacemaking in an increasingly public arena. Yet her call from God drew outrage from those who considered the public forum as man's domain. "Why is that woman gadding about so much? She's a woman. Why doesn't she stay in her cell, if it's God she wants to serve?"[7] Taunts such as these so

---

[4] *R* 2.1, pp. 116-17.

[5] *R* 2.1, p. 117.

[6] *Ibid.*

[7] *R* 3.4, p. 339.

cut at Catherine's heart that toward the end of her life she responded reluctantly even to the pope's request for her presence in Rome.

A letter to her friend Daniella, written perhaps a year or two before her death, gives some intimation of what her unreserved embracing of God's will had meant for Catherine. Vowed as a cloistered nun to the community at Orvieto, Daniella had been unable to escape the sense that God wanted her at Rome to support Urban in the crisis occasioned by two papal claimants. In the face of her own hesitation and the apparent opposition of her superiors she sought Catherine's advice.

Catherine's response hints at both the joy and pain which surrender to her own extraordinary call had brought her. She knew the suffering of obeying in silence when the directions of her confessors and superiors blocked her from pursuing what she believed God asked of her. Raymond describes her in these situations as "torn in two by an anguish which no word nor pen can picture."[8] Yet she confesses to Daniella that to feel "called by God in new ways" that seem closed to us delivers us to a bitter-sweet suffering which she herself had learned can render our hearts and wills even more receptive to God.

Catherine sensed that God had truly inspired Daniella's increased zeal and her willingness to sacrifice by going to Rome in service of the Church. She writes, however, that a decision so serious that it alters the course of our lives requires not only the counsel of holy and wise people, but also profound prayer and absolute trust that God will direct us and enlighten those responsible with us for the decision. On the other hand, love alone is absolute; every call in life is only a means, a "building" we lay on this foundation. Above all, we must be faithful to God through love. If God calls us to erect another building on this cornerstone and through fear of the risks involved we desert love in order to preserve

[8] *R* 1.9, pp. 74-75.75.

the original building, we close our hearts to God's will and choose infidelity of the deepest kind.

Catherine advises Daniella to consider the possibility of putting aside for a while the silence of cloistered life, lest the Lord chide her later for that silence when the Church needed voices to cry out the truth. As Catherine herself unfailingly had done, she urges Daniella to embrace God's will by obeying her superiors. She assures her friend that, whenever God's will rather than our own wishes is at stake, the Lord himself will change the hearts of those responsible with us for the decision and open the way for us in a manner that we would never have dreamed possible.[9]

The Spirit's Diverse Calls

Catherine realized that the more we understand how radically God has given himself to us, the more we want to be of one heart and will with him. And because the Holy Spirit is the very person of love, we say *yes* to God's will for us in proportion to our openness to the Spirit who draws us by paths of the most tender love. Often, we cannot see where these paths lead us or what sense they make until the journey itself is over and we find ourselves, often to our own amazement, safely home. When we look back at the unsuspected turns our lives have taken, when we see how perfectly God has embraced in the arms of his love even our missteps and refusals and turned them wondrously to our good, we cannot help desiring that the Spirit of mercy soften our resistance and render us absolutely receptive to God's gentle will for us in the future.

If we want to enter wholeheartedly into God's will for us, we need only ask the Spirit of God to embrace our lives, to inspire and lead us, to minister healing within us, and to so breathe love in us that we increasingly live, not out of the poverty of our own plans and resources, but out of the

---

[9]Let T 316.

Spirit's lavish and creative leading.[10] As Catherine prayed to her beloved Paul, she began to understand that embracing God's will means surrendering ourselves to this Spirit of mercy: "You joined your will with the Holy Spirit, loving perfectly that love that...was the reason for every grace given to you without your earning it" and whose only purpose was to "make you blessed and happy."[11] She learned, too, how the infinitely free Breath of God breathes where he will (Jn 3:8), refusing to be bound by our measures or to submit to our calculation and control. Her own call, which stood in opposition to all that seemed possible to women of her time, taught her that God's Spirit is not simply the giver of the rule but the rule itself, and that, when we long for God's will to be perfectly realized in us, we are in fact thirsting for unhindered openness to the Holy Spirit.[12]

As she ministered at the heart of the Church, Catherine recognized how truly the Church itself flourishes to the extent that the Spirit's unique calls and gifts to each person are encouraged. As the very person of love, the Spirit draws us away from self-sufficiency and so binds us to one another that we are unable to discern or live God's will in isolation. In this way, Catherine discovered the abyss of God's will as the infinite love uniting us to each other and manifesting the divine beauty and plenitude in our life together. When we impede God's call in others, therefore, we find ourselves

---

[10] Let T 64. William Flete of England, to whom this letter is addressed, was one of Catherine's most devoted disciples. A priest and scholar, he became enchanted with the woods at Lecceto ten miles away from Siena and asked his superiors for permission to make his home in them as a hermit. He had probably been a student at an English university, but according to Caffarini, cared nothing about the honors or advantages of gaining a doctorate. His learning and holiness made him known as the "bachelor of the Wood of the Lake." Because Lecceto was one of the holy places to which Catherine loved to make pilgrimages, she and William became close friends. He severely disappointed her, however, when he refused to leave his wood and join her in Rome in support of Urban VI. In this last context, Catherine's words to him about the will of God as a matter of the Spirit's leading rather than of personal preference take on special force.

[11] Pr 4, p. 43.

[12] Let T 294 to Sano di Maco and others at Siena.

resisting the Spirit of God.[13] In contrast, when we embrace God's will, we increasingly rejoice in the diverse calls among us, feeding one another with our unique gifts, and gladly encouraging diversity rather than conformity to a single path.[14] We travel life "royally," for, instead of judging others' intentions, we seek only God's will in everything.[15]

"In my Father's house there are many rooms" (Jn 14:2). Catherine loved to think of the joy we will experience in heaven as we see God's grandeur shining forth in the infinite variety among us. Each of us has been created as a singular sacrament of God's mercy, made to manifest in an unrepeatable manner an aspect of the triune God's splendor. As a unique creation of God's love, each of us travels also a singular path to holiness[16] marked by a special virtue that unifies our gifts and radiates charity in a distinctive way: "You guide your servants in different ways along different paths, ...Though they travel by different ways, they are all running along the fiery road of your charity."[17] In heaven we will understand how truly we embraced God's will by rejoicing in and encouraging the Spirit's diverse calls.[18]

---

[13]Let T 340. The woman to whom Catherine writes this letter, Agnesa da Toscanella, was noted for her great penances. We see here Catherine's focus on surrender to God's will and receptivity to others as well as to God, rather than the path of excessive penance, as the heart of holiness.

[14]*The Dialogue* 100; in Catherine of Siena, *The Dialogue,* translation and introduction by Suzanne Noffke, O.P. (New York: Paulist Press, 1980), p. 189. Future references to this work will be cited by the letter D with chapter, and page in Noffke's edition.

[15]Pr 9, p. 70.

[16]D 51, p. 104.

[17]Pr 9, pp. 69-70.

[18]Let T 39 to Don Iacomo. This Carthusian monk of the monastery of Pontignano near Siena was both a disciple of Catherine's and a good friend of her beloved secretary Stefano Maconi. He succeeded Stefano as prior of Pontignano.

The Path of Love Rather than Self-Will

As Catherine learned to love and to trust God's will for her, she saw how everything that comes from God's hand is "good and perfect."[19] Every vocation shines with the beauty and potential to foster the love which opens us to God,[20] for nothing human of itself is an obstacle to holiness. Spouse, family, responsibilities, possessions—if we embrace these gifts of God with generous love, we discover the very heart of holiness.[21] "It is an easy matter, for nothing is as easy and delightful as love." The Father's words to her convinced Catherine that every call is holy when lived with love: "What I ask of you is nothing other than love and affection for me and for your neighbors. This can be done at any time, any place, and in any state of life by loving."[22]

Through counseling others, Catherine began to understand that it is not our particular call in life that robs us of God, but rather our selfish way of loving the gifts of our call.[23] For God's love lavishes upon us unspeakable gifts of mercy at every second, but we often take these gifts for granted or love them in an unfree way, making them instead of God the focus of our hope. This selfishness that Catherine calls "self-will" blocks us from growing in true love and self-giving. She pictures God's gentle will as a beautiful garment that adorns and protects us, and our own selfish will as

---

[19]D 55, p. 110.

[20]Let T 193 to Lorenzo del Pino addresses one of the most famous lawyers of Catherine's time. He taught at the University of Bologna from 1365 until 1391, was an influential government leader, and one of four delegates sent to make peace with Pope Gregory XI. It was Lorenzo who responded in the name of Bologna to the representatives of the French papal claimant Clement VII, defending Bologna's loyalty to Urban VI. His writings included works related to civil and church law.

[21]Let T 259 to Tommaso d'Alviano, leader of an army of soldiers whom various heads of state enlisted in their battles against one another. He fought on the side of the Church against the Florentines in 1376, the apparent date of this letter.

[22]D 55, p. 110.

[23]Let T 193 to Lorenzo del Pino.

a "stinking" garment which leaves us alone and unprotected.[24]

Catherine gives a vivid description of this self-will as it leads us to a controlling and manipulative way of life and closes us off from the truth. When the "stinking garment" of self-will rules us, nothing is ever enough for us; instead of gratefully recognizing God's gifts to us in our state of life,[25] we relate to our spouse, children, friends, possessions, or work in a grasping and unfree way. Our endlessly frustrated desires and plans fill our lives with bitterness.[26] And instead of growing in personal autonomy and trust in God, we blame others for chains of our own making, experiencing in this way a foretaste of hell.[27]

In her letters to prosperous friends who wanted to live united to God's will, Catherine stresses the goodness of material possessions, for God wishes us to live in the joy of his gifts. Yet she also cautions that we can love these gifts in such a way that, instead of our possessing them, they begin to possess us. It is not created goods which keep us from God, then, but only our disordered way of loving them. And since no created reality can fully satisfy us, our selfish love costs us everything and leaves us with nothing.[28] When we

[24]Pr 11, pp. 87-88.

[25]Let T 116 to Monna Pantasilea da Farnese and Let T 299 to Ristoro Canigiani. Monna Pantasilea, wife of Ranuccio Farnese, whose brother Piero was a celebrated captain of the Florentine troops, stresses the path to holiness as accessible to all who live their lives in gratitude and love. Ristoro Canigiani, recipient of Let T 299, became a devoted follower of Catherine's. One of the most prestigious of Florence's noble families, Catherine's Canigiani disciples included Ristoro's father Piero, and his brother, Barduccio, who became Catherine's loved friend and secretary. Ristoro almost lost his life in the rioting that broke out in Florence in 1378 between the Guelphs, the popular party sympathetic to papal authority, and the Ghibellines, a rival aristocratic party. The Canigiani belonged to the ruling Guelphs and in the rioting incited by the Ghibellines, many Guelph families were massacred.

[26]Let T 55 to Don William, prior general of the Carthusians. His choice of allegiance to Clement VII rather than to Urban VI split the Carthusian Order until its reunion in 1410 when Stefano Maconi, Catherine's friend and secretary, became prior general.

[27]Let T 5 to Francesco da Montalcino, doctor of civil law.

[28]Let T 151 to Monna Nella Buonconti of Pisa.

love in this unfree way, we find that the more we have the more we want and yet the more empty we feel,[29] until envy robs us of joy even in what we do have.[30]

Catherine's experience in counseling others sharpened the distinction she saw between the goodness of material possessions and the two ways we can love them. When we cling selfishly to anyone or anything, we become enslaved to the very gifts God intended for our joy. As good as material possessions are, we will lose them all in death;[31] but when we love selfishly, even before death the pain of any loss assumes unbearable proportions for us.[32] In contrast, if we love everything as a gift lent to us by God's goodness,[33] our hearts grow secure in God's love and peace which no one can take from us, and so we experience even now a foretaste of heaven.[34]

As Catherine viewed the powerful civil and church leaders around her, she saw also how self-will can deceive us into thinking that we control others when actually we do not possess even our own selves.[35] The human prestige which Catherine calls the "world's smoke" easily deludes us into a false sense of power and complacency.[36] Catherine's own unsought influence showed her that we gain true power not by controlling others but by yielding ourselves to God in a

---

[29]Let T 237 (DT 79) to Louis, Duke of Anjou. This letter reflects Catherine's way of influencing the wealthy leader toward involvement in a crusade. King Charles V, brother of the Duke, had sent Louis to Avignon to counteract Catherine's authority in advising Gregory XI's return to Rome. The Duke, however, was so impressed with Catherine that he asked her to visit his castle at Villeneuve, ostensibly to direct him toward the path to holiness. Catherine encouraged Louis to undertake a crusade to the Holy Land as part of his dedication to God.

[30]D 48, p. 99.

[31]Let T 237 (DT 79) to Louis, Duke of Anjou.

[32]D 48, p. 99.

[33]Let T 193 to Lorenzo del Pino.

[34]Let T 299 to Ristoro Canigiani.

[35]Let T 259 to Tommaso d'Alviano.

[36]Let T 256 to Niccolò, prior of the province of Tuscany.

love that respects others.[37] Her own busy life taught her also that what makes our lives valuable is not selfish absorption in our own projects, but the generous love which embraces God's will. The true lifework of each of us is love.[38] And because love's interior power extends far beyond what our limited energies can achieve, the work we do out of love, even if it fails, will surely endure.[39]

In sharp contrast to her account of our selfish will's "stinking garment," Catherine describes the "lightsome garment" of God's will for us in the most bright and joyful of images. This "gentle will," like the sun, shines its radiance on the barren earth of our being, coaxing us with its light and warmth into the most marvelous fruitfulness.[40] The more we yield ourselves to this sun's warmth, the more we find ourselves truly home, planted in the most welcoming garden of God's will.[41] We will know that we have made our home in this will when we no longer want to have anything in our own way, but only in God's way.[42] But if we cling to our own will, we find ourselves weak and unprotected, for our efforts come to nothing when we try to flourish outside the gracious strength of God's will: "Out of your own will you created ours, and . . . ours is strong when it dwells in yours."[43] As we learn this truth by experience, we begin to let no other light except God's own will shine upon us: "She closes her will so that it loves nothing outside of you."[44]

---

[37]Let T 28 (DT 17) to Bernabò Visconti of Milan, one of the most ruthless men of Catherine's time. A person of great valor and culture—he founded the University of Pisa—he was also known for his unspeakable cruelty, and died in prison after being dethroned by his nephew.

[38]Let T 38 to Monna Agnesa Malavolti.

[39]Let T 213 to Suor Daniella da Orvieto.

[40]Pr 11, p. 89.

[41]Pr 3, p. 39.

[42]Pr 11, p. 88.

[43]Pr 14, p. 122.

[44]Pr 15, p. 131.

Discretion

But how can we learn to distinguish between the impulses of our own selfish will and the light and warmth of God's will for us? Catherine's call and temperament made her sensitive to how easily we try to impose our own way even on God. She discovered that openness to God's will needs "discretion," the discernment that comes from love and that opens us to the unique invitations of God in each person and situation. Because God's will is nothing but love, we embrace this will when through discretion we choose what best fosters love in each circumstance. Love, in turn, gives us even clearer eyes to see and to discern God's will, while discernment itself makes us more patient, gentle, and receptive to God and others.[45]

Having suffered herself from people's attempts to control her life and activity, Catherine stresses the importance of leading and guiding others with discretion, since our selfish will can be particularly destructive when we serve in positions of responsibility. Instead of freeing others, the way we exercise authority can imprison them.[46] But if we lead with discretion, we can enable others to grow in openness not to our will but to God's will for them.[47]

Catherine recognized also the need for discretion in confronting another's fault. She pictures love's discernment as opening our eyes to the same weakness in ourselves that we see in others. When people find themselves "so gently understood," they will often acknowledge themselves the very fault we wished to point out to them and will change all the more willingly. In this way discretion gives us the discernment of love, especially when we are called to speak truth that is difficult.[48]

---

[45]Let T 213 to Suor Daniella of Orvieto.

[46]*Ibid.*

[47]Let T 65 to Suor Daniella of Orvieto.

[48]D 102, pp. 193-94.

Compassion

Critical and self-willed by nature, Catherine learned by experience how mercy and compassion foster receptivity to God's will in our lives. In her youth she had lacerated her body, but as a mature woman she learned to yield her whole being to the greater power of interior love and mercy. This was no easy lesson for her; she confesses to her friend Daniella her difficulty in living the truth she preached to others: "I feel that I have often fallen into irritation and a judicial attitude toward my neighbor."[49]

Catherine recalls the Father's words to her in the *Dialogue:* "Nothing in the world can make it right for you to sit in judgment on the intention" of others..."If you do you will be deluded in your judgment. But compassion is what you must have, you and the others, and leave the judging to me."[50] As she suffered from others' misunderstanding and criticism, Catherine grew to understand that we see only the appearances, while God sees the heart (1 Sam 16:7); we look at people's faults, but God looks at their struggle and desire for good. If we ourselves try to see with the eyes of God's love, we can learn to focus on others' goodness rather than on their failings, and, in this way, turn our judgment into one of mercy and God's own compassion.[51]

Convinced that infinite love draws good for us from every trial, Catherine herself tried to dwell on God's love rather than on people's unkindness to her.[52] Raymond recounts how she had only to appear in public to pray and she would be the butt of every kind of joke and abuse on the part of those who mistrusted her. Jealous sisters of the *mantellate* so poisoned the Dominican friars against her that the priests would frequently refuse to give her the Eucharist or to hear

---

[49]Let T 65; in *St. Catherine of Siena as Seen in Her Letters,* translated and edited with introduction by Vida D. Scudder (New York: E. P. Dutton and Co., 1927), p. 70.

[50]D 105, p. 197.

[51]Let T 307 to a woman in Siena.

[52]D 100, p. 191.

her confession. When she spent long hours in church absorbed in prayer, women would kick her and the friars would "throw her out of the church like so much refuse."[53] And yet, Raymond comments, Catherine profited from every one of these experiences.[54]

In response to her prayer, the Lord gave Catherine his own will. Raymond himself noticed how after this mystical experience Catherine grew increasingly content with all that God permitted in her life.[55] Yet this contentment entailed no irresponsible and passive stance in the face of wrongs; on the contrary, she worked all the more passionately for peace and justice. But when her efforts seemed to bear no fruit, she would choose inner peace rather than rancor, trusting that God would accomplish justice far more through her compassion than through anger. "O lovely compassion...you are a balm that snuffs out rage and cruelty in the soul. This compassion, compassionate Father, I beg you to give to all."[56] Her own life taught her that the weakness we condemn today in another is the sin into which we ourselves will fall tomorrow unless God's grace preserves us. Once we experience the depth of this truth in our lives, the openness to God's will which only compassion can foster begins to bestow its beauty and fragrance everywhere around us.[57]

Embracing God's Will in Trial: The Bitter Becomes Sweet

"It is only in patience that you will possess your souls" (Lk 21:19). Catherine's impetuous and ardent temperament both caused her a continual struggle with anger and impatience and prompted her to pray constantly for the gift of increased

[53]R 3.6, pp. 370-71.
[54]R 2.5, p. 171.
[55]R 2.6, p. 183.
[56]Pr 15, p. 134.
[57]D 100, pp. 190-91.

receptivity to God's will. At the heart of her difficulties, the gift of God's own peace and joy filled her with growing contentment in the face of all that God permitted in her life.[58] In prayer she grew to understand that our deepest joy in heaven will be flourishing in the glad abyss of the Father's will and that we can taste this sweetness even now through the inner calm that drinks in God's goodness everywhere. We then begin to know how truly embracing God's will through love not only frees us but also anoints our lives with peace.[59]

Yet how can we become content with God's will in the face of sufferings which evoke from us only anger and resentment? A friend writes to ask Catherine this question, grieved that in the trial he is enduring, he feels only rebellion rather than desire for God's will. Catherine assures him that our very concern about God's will shows that we have already embraced this will at a deep level of our beings. In the midst of tragedy, we cannot escape the need to work through feelings of anger and bitterness. Yet even if we feel no desire for God's will, if we feel nothing at all, our concern about that will evidences our desire for it at an unspoken level more profound than our negative feelings.[60]

"We know that in everything God works for good with those who love him" (Rom 8:28). Catherine endured tragedy herself and suffered with friends as they grieved bitter losses. But her own experience taught her that even the most cruel sufferings hide within them the tenderness of God's will and the treasure of his infinite love.[61] As she reflected on the meaning of our pain in the light of Jesus' own death, she found that under the "bitter rind," a "sweet fruit" lies hidden; God can draw forth even from the ashes of our broken lives the most radiant joy and new life. If we pray for the grace not to resist God's "sweet will," the Lord's own love can heal

[58]Let T 335 to Don Cristofano, Carthusian monk.

[59]D 151, p. 322.

[60]Let T 17 to Frate Antonio da Nizza, Augustinian hermit at Selva di Lago.

[61]Let T 335 to Don Cristofano, Carthusian monk.

our wounds and free our hearts for even deeper growth.[62]

We know how painful it is to endure a tragedy over which we have no control. Yet like the orange whose hard and bitter rind hides the sweet fruit within, our pain when embraced by God's love hides within it an unspeakably sweet outcome. "Deliver yourself to this sweet bitterness," Catherine writes; patience rather than rebellion yields the fruit of inestimable peace and growth for us.[63] When we live united with God's will, no pain can ever destroy us, for God's love gives us a peace the world cannot bestow, a peace that lasts until death and beyond it.[64]

Our maturity and openness to God grow and deepen through the unavoidable sufferings of life. As she comforted her friend Mona Agnese during a time of tragic loss, Catherine stressed this truth, for she sensed how precious her friend was to God; every tie that could bind her to earth had been cut away. In the midst of tragedy we gradually gain the freedom of heart that no longer clings to anything but Jesus.[65] Like the doctor who allows us bitter remedies to heal us, God ministers to our inner wounds by permitting us loss. Through enduring these sufferings, we face the strength of our own selfish will and so all the more want God's freeing will to take hold of us.[66] If we ask for the grace to say *yes* when the bonds that hold us fast are loosened, we gain a freedom that lets us run unhindered to increasingly deeper dimensions of life. Cut off from the controlling influence even of our own selfish will, we have no bridle left to block us from growing in love and freedom.[67] This freedom is ours when we no longer want our way but God's way for us: "This is the surest sign that people are clothed in your will:

[62]Let T 151 to Monna Nella Buonconti of Pisa.

[63]Let T 346 to Pope Urban VI.

[64]D 131, p. 263.

[65]Let T 38 to Monna Agnesa Malavolti.

[66]Let T 264 to Monna Iacoma Trinci of Fuligno.

[67]Let T 132 (DT 48) possibly to Cecca di Clemente Gori and others of the *Mantellate* in Siena.

that they see the cause of events in your will not in human will" and that they see adversity as "motivated only by love."[68]

Catherine loved to picture Jesus himself not only embracing the cross but even running to it like one insane with love. Held fast to the cross not by nails but by the unbounded love which he had and still has for us, Jesus nurtured one burning desire, that he would accomplish his Father's will. How, then, can we ourselves "lift up our head against the goodness of God," and wish that our narrow will would be accomplished? "How shall we not will that the will of God be fulfilled?"[69]

"Come to me, all who labor and are heavy burdened and I will give you rest...for my yoke is easy and my burden is light" (Mt 11:28-30). Catherine continues to invite her loved ones "from the depths of her heart" to the well-springs of the patience she saw described in these Gospel verses. "Full of joy and peace," patience flourishes as the best loved daughter of charity, since it bears all things in love. Under its "sweet yoke" we find our peace, for every human bitterness finally becomes sweet in the expansive delight of God's will.[70]

Embracing the Will of God: Love's Transforming Power

Imperious and self-willed: more than a few of her contemporaries would have described Catherine this way. She suffered, it is true, from the criticism of people who misunderstood and mistrusted her, yet their criticism more than once bore its own measure of truth. The strength of Catherine's will was her greatest asset, but it was also her deep cross.

---

[68] Pr 2, p. 25.

[69] Let T 132 (DT 48) to *Mantellate* in Siena; Scudder, p. 99.

[70] Let T 68 to Benedetta de' Belforti of Volterra, whose husband, the tyrant Bocchino de' Belforti, was murdered in 1411.

Admonitions to her friends to grow in patience and reverence before life's trials, injunctions to love and to embrace "the sweet will of God:" these pleas of Catherine to others betray the extent of her own struggle. It cost her deeply to yield unreservedly to God an ardent temperament that was also critical, impatient and self-willed.

Catherine was no stranger to the desire for control. She recognized, painfully so, the contrast between her characteristic *Io voglio,* "I will it," and the words attributed to Jesus: "My food is to do the will of him who sent me" (Jn 4:34). As Catherine watched the havoc that her own will and plans could cause, she gradually learned to choose instead the life and freedom of God's will. From the moment that the Lord answered her prayer by giving her his own will, Catherine became "content with everything that happened" in her life; her presence bespoke a serenity and joy that seemed never to leave her.[71]

The discovery that she could gain her life only by letting go of it (Mt 10:39) literally changed the course of her life. In her own will she had found the narrow world of a single self, but in God's will she gained communion with the joy and pain of the whole world. She discovered, too, her gifts blossoming in their most creative potential for making an impact on the world. Clothed in God's will, the unschooled Catherine found within herself the resources to preach and to write with a clarity and depth that earned for her the title of doctor of the Church.

In company with Mary, Catherine learned to say with her life, "I am the handmaid of the Lord; let it be to me according to your word" (Lk 1:38). In doing so, Catherine experienced the "fragrance" of a patience and peace that never left her. By embracing God's will she found the love that so transformed her into "another himself"[72] that she became content with all that God's tender mercy does and permits.[73]

---

[71] R 2.6, p. 183.

[72] D 1, p. 26.

[73] Let T 116 to Monna Pantalisea da Farnese.

The "very sweet balm of peace" that only God's will can give taught her how to receive everything with reverence.[74] And whether the world wanted to or not, it could not help respecting one whom love had transformed[75] in the way she herself had described in prayer: "O dispossessed will, earnest of eternal life! You are faithful even to the point of death.... not to the world but to your most gentle Creator. And you bind the soul to him because she has been completely freed from herself."[76]

In a letter to a close friend Catherine prays that like Mary she will not only embrace God's will but finally be embraced by this will. From the depths of her own life which unfolded in the abyss of God's will more wondrously than she herself could have imagined, Catherine surely continues to offer this prayer in the name of each person close to her: "Oh Jesus, gentlest love, let your will be done in us always as it is in heaven by your angels and saints!"[77]

---

[74]Let T 359 to Leonardo Frescobaldi of Florence.

[75]Let T 215 to certain monasteries in Bologna.

[76]Pr 11, p. 88.

[77]Let T 132 (DT 48) to *Mantellate* in Siena; in the forthcoming Volume I of *The Letters of Catherine of Siena,* general editor, Suzanne Noffke, O.P.

3

Clothed in the Truth

"For this I was born, and for this I have come into the world, to bear witness to the truth" (Jn 18:37). The reader of Catherine's writings soon becomes aware of how completely this scriptural insight took hold of her. The will of God had called her to be a passionate word of truth in the world, and everything in her was made to respond without reserve. Wherever she found it, truth drew her with such irresistible force that to deny it would have been to deny her very being. Against the backdrop of the lies and confusion that marked the age in which she lived, Catherine herself became a crystal clear word, a living sacrament of truth's power to draw the human mind and heart with its beauty.

In the clear and unambiguous word of Jesus' person, where all of the promises of God find their *yes* (2 Cor 1:19-20), Catherine discovered the Father's perfectly transparent image (Col 1:15). "I am...the truth" (Jn 14:6): Catherine's own thirst for clarity led her to Jesus in whose radiance she found the ultimate meaning and beauty of all truth.

Truth That Will Not Fail Us

As we read of Catherine's passion for truth, the question placed by the Johannine author on the lips of Pilate—"What is truth?" (Jn 18:8)—inevitably wells up from our own minds and hearts. Experience itself teaches us how we thirst for truth more deeply than we are able to articulate its meaning; at the core of our beings we reach out for the clarity of what is real, for the transparency of what is rather than the illusion of what pretends to be. We know the spontaneous cry of inner joy when we finally "see" the meaning of something we have not understood, or when another's words strike a deep chord in our heart. And when the world around us is as we sense it ought to be, we feel the power of truth to fill us not only with what is real, but also with what is beautiful.

But even as we know the tender and exquisite joys of life that satisfy us with truth's beauty, we know, too, the reality of broken relationships, of institutions and investments which have failed us. In the midst of life's gladness, the betrayal of others and our own infidelity at times force us by their pain to question whether there is anything or anyone worthy of trust or finally true in the world. Catherine herself knew life's deceptions even as she experienced its gifts. With her own hands she buried loved nieces and nephews, victims of the Plague. People she selflessly nursed and others for whom she negotiated peace turned against her; the pride and cowardice of trusted Church leaders inaugurated a schism that split Christendom apart. Catherine lived in a Church and world that had learned how to make peace with lies.

Yet everything in her thirsted for the radiance and passion of truth. Her letters, tender when dealing with weakness, are unsparing toward the consciously chosen lie. Cardinals who had repudiated Pope Urban VI felt the force of Catherine's anger with their deception; the solemnity with which they had carried out his coronation proved the truth they could not deny "except with plain lies." "On what side soever," she writes, "I find nothing but lies." The cardinals corrupt the truth and proclaim that Urban is the anti-pope; "But anyone who says it—speaking to you without reverence, because you have deprived yourself of reverence—lies up to his eyes."[1]

In the experience of betrayals such as these, Catherine learned the depth of our human desire for integrity rather than deception, for as surely as our bodies need air and water, our spirits crave the truth. Yet we often discover the elusive meaning and beauty of truth only through the crushing experience of a lie; only after we have been deceived do we learn how deeply we cannot live without truth. With emptiness as its only content, a lie can never deliver to the human spirit what is real; promising everything and delivering nothing, a lie pretends to be and is not, so that even when it seems to hold out what is good, it is always an enemy.

The God of all being, however, has made us not for illusions and shadows, but for what is real. Truth is the radiant transparency of this reality, the attachment of the human spirit not to what pretends to be but to what is. But we sometimes give ourselves over to lies precisely because we fear the pain of life's truth. In her own sufferings, however, Catherine began to recognize that every truth of our lives exists at the heart of an infinitely more merciful reality, the truth of God who loved us before we were made and who embraces within his goodness our own meaning and destiny. In the midst of lies and betrayal, Catherine learned to trust that this ultimate truth gives meaning to every partial truth that seems able to destroy us. For Catherine, there does exist a final truth that will not fail us, a truth whose tenderness and gladness heal and redeem every reality in the universe.[2] For this reason the Father tells Catherine, "I want you to be a lover of all things, because everything is good, perfect, and

---

[1] Let T 310 to three Italian cardinals; Scudder, pp. 280, 279. These three cardinals, who at first acknowledged Urban as pope and then turned their allegiance to Clement VII, were Pietro Corsini of Florence, Simon de Borgono of Milan, and Iacomo Orsini of Rome.

[2] D 21, p. 58.

worthy of love. I, supreme Goodness, made them all—all but sin."[3]

When anguish and confusion rob us of peace, this ultimate truth of God's love lightens the burdens and sweetens the bitterness in our lives.[4] Precisely because God is ever "more ready to pardon than we are to sin," we must never lose sight of how "beloved of God" we are.[5] If we take time to remember forgotten blessings, we discover the truth no power in the universe can destroy, the infinite love that is ours in the blood of Jesus.[6] And we know this truth not through visions or revelations but through the darkness of faith that trusts in the mercy which Jesus' blood pours upon us.[7] The God of the universe has shed his blood for *me*.[8] The power of this truth calls us from discouragement and despair to hope and new life: "So we ought to fill our memory with this glorious blood, which shows us so sweet a truth."[9]

The Cloud of Selfish Love

The wars and schism dividing Christendom during her lifetime convinced Catherine that selfishness above all se-

[3]Let T 30 (DT 1) to the Abbess and Suora Niccolosa of the Monastery of Santa Marta in Siena; Noffke, trans.

[4]Let T 282 to Nicola da Osimo, secretary to Gregory XI.

[5]Let T 178 to Neri di Landoccio dei Pagliaresi, Catherine's beloved friend and secretary; Scudder, p. 95. Neri's sensitive nature made him prey to bouts of depression and discouragement, but Catherine was ever ready to lighten his spirit with her kindness. She frequently sent Neri as her emissary to Gregory XI and Urban VI as well as to the Queen of Naples. After Catherine's death, Neri lived as a hermit.

[6]Let T 362 to Giovanna d'Angio, Queen of Naples, who evoked both affection and impatience from Catherine. The queen's reputation for wickedness inspired Catherine's attempts to win her over to Jesus, but when the monarch changed her loyalty to Clement VII, Catherine's ire equaled her affection. Married four times, Giovanna was strangled on May 22, 1382—an end that bespoke the cruelty of much of her own life.

[7]Let T 227 to William Flete.

[8]Let T 178 to Neri di Landoccio.

[9]Let T 93 to Monna Orsa Usimbardi and Monna Agnese di Pipino; Scudder, p. 75.

duces us away from the truth into living a lie.[10] "Blindness upon blindness, which does not let its wrong be seen nor the loss to soul and body!" "Had you seen it," Catherine writes to Church leaders, "you would not have deserted the truth so lightly, in servile fear. . . What made you do this?" The "poison" of selfishness.[11] Our creation through love makes us unable to live without love, but when we selfishly cling to what is not God, our desire for love fastens itself to a lie. If we saw clearly, however, we would recognize that "from such a love as this naught can result but pain."[12]

Selfishness can become a "cloud" that so blocks out from our world anything but ourselves that we begin to use other people rather than to treasure them as gifts of God's love to us. The lie of selfishness in this way seduces and enslaves us to what, in the end, will inevitably fail us. Experience itself teaches us how tortured our lives become when we love honor and power, people and possessions in a grasping, unfree way.[13] In this way selfishness begins to act like a cloud around us, pushing away from us the truth that nothing created can be God for us, and opening us to a living hell on earth.[14] Lies appear to be truth to us and truth appears to be a lie;[15] the bitter seems sweet and the good seems bitter.[16] Like an insidious poison, selfishness ultimately deceives us into thinking that transitory satisfactions have the power to calm our yearnings.[17]

[10]Let T 296 to Don Giovanni of the Cells.

[11]Let T 310 to three Italian cardinals; Scudder, pp. 281, 278.

[12]*Ibid.;* Scudder, p. 276.

[13]Let T 193 to Lorenzo del Pino of Bologna.

[14]Let T 299 to Ristoro Canigiani.

[15]Let T 307 to a woman at Siena.

[16]Let T 315 to Don Pietro da Milano, Carthusian monk.

[17]Let T 310 to three Italian cardinals.

"You Will Know the Truth and the Truth Will Make You Free" (Jn 8:31)

The Sienese fiercely loved freedom and Catherine shared their passion, but she also recognized how we who crave bodily freedom easily give ourselves to a far more tyrannical interior master. We are slaves when the true motivation for our life is other than the deepest place within us, when our actions choose one reality while our inner beings choose another. But as we learn to make decisions from within our personal autonomy in God rather than from internal or external constraint, we begin to know true freedom; we are liberated when the source of our decisions lies within us, when our actions flow from our deepest identity in God.

In the confusion and deception surrounding her, Catherine saw how easily we forfeit our freedom and enslave ourselves to lies precisely when we most need to live the truth.[18] And when we live the emptiness of a lie, doubt and fear attach themselves to us as our constant companions: "If you know and love the truth, you will not fear pain..., otherwise, your shadow will make you afraid."[19] Enslaved to desires that can never fulfill us, we become caught in chains of our own making as our selfishness imprisons us in fears that attack us from every side—fears of not gaining what we want and fears of losing what we already have.

But when we live in the truth, no prison of illusion or deception contains us; we run unhindered in the open meadows of the infinitely true and real love of God for us. Unlike selfishness, God's love so increases our confidence that we learn to fear no created power. As she urges Queen Giovanna of Naples to support Pope Urban VI, Catherine reminds her that only the truth can give us this kind of radical inner freedom:[20] "You will know the truth and the truth will make you free" (Jn 8:31). By grounding us in the

---

[18] Let T 299 to Ristoro Canigiani.

[19] Let T 284 to Cardinal Pietro di Luna of Spain, who met Catherine at Avignon and with whom Raymond of Capua often dealt.

[20] Let T 317 to Giovanna d'Angio, Queen of Naples.

divine love that enfolds the universe, the truth heals our
confusions and fears and anchors us in what is most real and
powerful. We then learn to bind ourselves and others with
chains not of fear and manipulation but of mercy and charity. Fastened in this way to God and to our brothers and
sisters with the bonds of love, we experience the power of
truth not only to make us free but also to keep us free.[21]

Sea of Truth and Love

As her travels took her out of Siena to cities located near
the coast, Catherine learned to treasure the mystery hinted at
in the sea. The more she gazed at the water's beauty, the
more she was drawn to experience it, to enter it, to feel the
mystery of its depths. She realized that the more deeply she
would plunge into its abyss, the more she would discover its
hidden beauty; the more she would find of its alluring treasures, the more she would want to find. The vast body of
water whose mystery overwhelmed her with awe began to
speak to her of God.

The Trinity became for Catherine a "deep sea" that she
sought to enter with all the powers of her being: "The more I
enter you, the more I discover, and the more I discover, the
more I seek you."[22] She wondered at the miracle of this
attraction in her to the truth of God, flowing spontaneously
from within her own being, not wrenched out of her by a
force outside herself. In the dynamic of truth giving birth to
love Catherine began to recognize our human beauty and
dignity in their ultimate freedom. She thus invites Queen
Giovanna of Naples, whom she loved tenderly despite her
wickedness, to choose the truth courageously so that she
would freely love it.[23] And she reminds her friend, the hermit
and scholar William Flete of England, "The one who does

---

21 *Ibid.*

22 D 167, p. 364.

23 Let T 362 to Giovanna, Queen of Naples.

not know cannot love. The one who knows, loves."[24]

The mystery of water became for Catherine an image of God in another way. Water is made to be felt and tasted; we love to plunge ourselves into its refreshing depths, to drink in its goodness, to quench our thirst with its loveliness. "As the deer longs for the fountain of living water, so does my soul long...to see you in truth;" these words of Psalm 42 Catherine made her own. As she increasingly recognized in truth itself the fountain of living water (Jn 4:14) to which the Lord invites us, her passion for God became a thirst for the truth of God. Because truth alone gives rise to love, she longed to know the truth that would plunge her unendingly into the abyss of God's love: "You are insatiable, you in whose depths the soul is sated yet remains always hungry for you, thirsty for you, eternal Trinity."[25]

In this central insight, that we can love only what we know, Catherine grounded her entire life and spirituality. For her, the truth is not separate from the abyss of God's love; the truth *is* this abyss. And just as truth gives birth to love, love itself gives birth to truth, opening our eyes to dimensions of reality which would otherwise remain closed to us. For this reason Catherine urges her beloved friend and secretary Neri to "contemplate the truth in the abyss of divine charity."[26]

Catherine began to understand also that just as light enables us to see, only an "inner light" opens us to the truth.[27] Reason, the light for our minds, allows us to walk free and not as slaves or animals, while the light of faith given in Baptism enables us to grasp greater depths of life than what merely human sight can fathom. The most powerful light, however, is God's gift to those who love, for love knows the truth through an experiential or "love-knowing." Love itself thus becomes a light in us that illumines "the unspeakable

---

[24]Let T 77 to William Flete.

[25]D 167, p. 364.

[26]Let T 46 to Neri di Landoccio Pagliaresi.

[27]Let T 310 to three Italian cardinals.

love of God" for us, while knowledge in turn inspires and breaks forth into still deeper love. Truth and love in this way continually and inseparably give birth to deeper levels of one another: "Love follows upon understanding. The more they know, the more they love, and the more they love, the more they know. Thus each nourishes the other."[28]

Spirit of Truth

The Johannine author recounts the promise of Jesus: "I will pray the Father and he will give you another Counselor, to be with you forever, even the Spirit of truth...you know him, for he dwells with you, and will be in you" (Jn 14:16-17). In the Spirit, living Breath of God who inflamed the hearts and illumined the minds of the apostles at Pentecost, Catherine discovered the source of light in those who love. "God's love has been poured into our hearts through the Holy Spirit who has been given to us" (Rom 5:5). Augustine knew the Spirit as the living person of love, the mutual joy and delight of the Father and Son, while Bernard of Clairveaux named the Spirit as the embrace and kiss of the Father and Son. Catherine experienced this same Spirit as the person of love who imparts light and depth-understanding to those who love.

As much as she gained from humble scholars, Catherine knew also the scorn of proud intellectuals, the criticism of "foolish, proud, and learned" people whose pride had blotted out the Spirit's light in them. "Chasing after a multiplicity of books" without love, the proud often gain less knowledge of truth than the unschooled who possess the Spirit's light as the fruit of love. For this reason, Catherine stresses that even the most uneducated may bear the light of truth with the greatest clarity and depth, for in yielding to the

[28]D 85, p. 157.

Spirit, "they possess the chief source of that light from which learning comes."[29]

Because the Spirit's love breaks forth as a light within us, the more we invite the Holy Spirit to reign within us, the more our learning will lead us to knowledge not simply of facts but of truth. Catherine was convinced that we are aided in this search for truth only by those who, whether educated or—like Catherine herself—unschooled, are submitted to God's Spirit. "It is far better to walk by the spiritual counsel of a humble and unschooled person with a holy and upright conscience than by that of a well-read but proud scholar with great knowledge," for true lovers of God "share the light within them in hunger and longing for others' salvation."[30]

And as we ourselves surrender more deeply to God, we begin to experience love as an inner light and vision enabling us to see and understand far more than our reason alone could know. Since love of its nature dissolves alienation and separation by increasingly uniting us to the one loved, holy women and men throughout the ages have known the truth only through yielding to the Holy Spirit, God's love in person. Catherine herself savored the interior word of God to her about this depth-union which love effects: "And if anyone should ask me what this soul is, I would say: She is another me, made so by the union of love." The radiance of love's union shines as a light "lovely beyond all loveliness." And because not even the person's will stands as a divisive force between her and God,[31] the clarity of truth gained through love far exceeds what study without love can achieve.

Those who make the choice to love continue to radiate the truth in myriads of ways: "Your eternal truth offers the truth in different ways to different people...according to their

[29] *Ibid.*
[30] *Ibid.*
[31] D 96, p. 181.

different dispositions."[32] In every epoch women and men yielded to God's Spirit have thus shared uniquely in the one light of love and have borne God's truth to the world in complementary ways.[33] Paul learned the saving truth not from human teachers but from the Spirit of love,[34] while John drank in truth at the breast of Christ, Truth itself. And in the union of love doctors of the Church like Aquinas not only gained their deepest insights but also learned to transform their knowledge into the "fragrance" of intercession and preaching that cried out for the world's salvation.[35]

Spouse of the Truth

Catherine's own experience taught her that passion for the truth of God pushes us to the heart of the world where we allow the pain and suffering of our brothers and sisters to become our own. Because truth's ultimate meaning manifests itself in the concrete reality of the world's redemption, Catherine understood that we must proclaim the truth not because it is interesting but because it is saving truth. She thus writes to her cloistered friend Daniella of Orvieto that we who taste in prayer and study the fire of God's truth and love for us are inescapably called to rise up impassioned for the world's healing.[36]

Yet selfishness can so block our freedom with fear that we shrink from speaking the truth or we dilute the truth with lies and evasions. The schism caused by two papal claimants only intensified Catherine's ardent plea for the reign of truth. She penned scores of letters to Church and civil rulers, urging them to act with "virile hearts," as servants of God freed from the hypocrisy which bears in their hearts one reality

---

[32]Pr 21, p. 193.

[33]D 85, p. 156.

[34]D 83, p. 152.

[35]D 96, p. 181.

[36]Let T 316 to Suora Daniella da Orvieto.

and on their tongues another.[37] Only by boldly living and
proclaiming the truth will we know true freedom, for lies so
debase our dignity that we begin to live in fear of our own
shadows:[38] "Have courage....The truth is our strength.
Fear nothing, for the truth sets us free."[39] Even to her close
friend, Raymond, Catherine finds it necessary to write,
"Courage, become a good instrument..., announce the
truth generously."[40]

Catherine recalls the days of Pentecost. The apostles'
cowardice led them to flee their Lord, denying that they had
ever known him; the friends closest to Jesus abandoned him
to the hands of his enemies. But when the Spirit of truth
came upon them, their eyes were opened to the saving truth;
they saw the contrast between the world's empty strength
before which they had cowered and the power of God's love
which had embraced them in Jesus. At that moment,
"through love they lost their fear."[41]

As she thought of the radical transformation which love
had achieved in the apostles, Catherine began to reflect on
the spouse whom love makes unafraid, for "perfect love casts
out fear" (1 Jn 4:18). The one who desires only the beloved's
good increasingly lives free of fear, with a love so committed
that it would die for the spouse. Catherine became convinced that God invites each of us to the same kind of passionate love that transforms us into a "spouse of the truth."
She saw that since every reality outside of God's truth has
only the pretense of power, the spouse of truth learns to fear
no one but God. If silence must be guarded, therefore, we do

[37]Let T 364 to Pope Urban VI.

[38]Let T 361 to a confidante of the Queen of Naples.

[39]Let T 347 to Conte Alberico da Balbiano, captain general of the Company of
St. George and other leaders. As captain general of the Company of St. George,
Conte Alberico led a troop of four thousand whose efforts freed Rome of the
onslaughts of Clement VII's army. His loyalty to Urban did not last, however, and
he eventually transferred his allegiance to the very man whose army he had routed
from Rome.

[40]Let T 226 to Raymond of Capua.

[41]Let T 94 to Frate Matteo di Francesco Tolomei, O.P.; Scudder, p. 87.

not speak; but if truth must be proclaimed, nothing can keep us silent. "Cry out as if you had a million voices," she urges; "It is silence which kills the world."[42] "Proclaim the truth and do not be silent through fear."[43] And when we learn not only to speak the truth but also to wed our entire life to truth, we will discover, as the apostles did, the indescribable joy of living free of fear.[44]

Truth as Our Clothing

As her writings so unmistakably show, Catherine clung to truth, not as an arid world of abstract ideas, but as the most real of all reality, the love which founds the universe. In the truth of God, where every form of death is robbed of its victory, she found the ultimate value of human life in its pain and joy. She became convinced that only when truth reigns in our lives will we know the inestimable meaning and beauty of human freedom.

Catherine's passion for truth was inseparable from her mystical intuition into its saving power; her thirst for truth became identically a passion for the world's redemption. In the fiber of her life Catherine grew "restless with tremendous desire for God's honor and the salvation of souls" because love's affection had made her "another himself;" possessed by love, she sought to "clothe herself" with truth.[45] Dominic's fiery preaching of truth had one purpose, to claim the world for the joy of God's love. As she prayed daily in the Dominican church of Siena, Catherine internalized in a profound way the motto of Dominic's Order, *Veritas,* as Dominic's mission of fire became her own passion.

Because she had discovered in Jesus the living person of saving truth, Catherine never tired of urging those she loved,

[42]Let T 16 to a great prelate.

[43]Let T 330 to Raymond of Capua.

[44]Let T 275 to Raymond of Capua.

[45]D 1, p. 25.

"choose the truth...; will to know the truth!"[46] She had learned that both the path of lies and that of truth beckon us; both paths are difficult, and both are possible. But while the path of lies opens us to bitterness and emptiness, to confusion and slavery, the path of God's truth leads us to sweetness and strength, to clarity and freedom.[47]

If we make the choice for truth in our lives we begin to discover a mysterious paradox; knowing the truth, we love it, and loving it, we are "clothed in it" with a power stronger than any other force.[48] The *Dialogue* which begins with Catherine's plea to know the truth ends with her cry of gratitude for this gift bestowed. The warmth and passion of truth assume for Catherine the proportions of a glorious garment clothing us in light and goodness: "Good above every good..., You, garment who cover all nakedness, pasture the starving within your sweetness."[49]

Catherine in this way pictures truth as the clothing we wear, for clothing both protects our skin and on a deeper level speaks who we are. Our clothing is in some sense we ourselves spoken aloud, the outward transparency of our inward selves. When we are not at peace with who we are, the way we present ourselves exteriorly contradicts who we are interiorly. But when we are at peace with ourselves, our clothing discloses outwardly our inward identity. "Clothed in the truth," we are free; there is no need for pretense or lies, for evasions and cover-ups that say one thing while we are and mean another. Truth itself becomes the clothing that extends our inward identity out into the world around us so that who we are can be a gift to others as well: "Such a heart is so open that it is false to no one; everyone can understand it because it never says something different with its face or tongue from what it has within."[50]

[46]Let T 305 to Pope Urban VI; Scudder, p. 287.

[47]D 28, p. 67.

[48]Let T 305 to Pope Urban VI.

[49]D 167, p. 366.

[50]Pr 15, p. 132.

At the end of her *Dialogue,* Catherine breaks forth in a hymn of praise to God for the unspeakable gift of truth: "Who could reach to your height to thank you for so immeasurable a gift..., for the teaching of truth that you have given me?... You willed to bend down to my need and that of others who might see themselves mirrored here."[51] Catherine knew that her passion for truth mirrors the yearning deep in every human heart to live in clarity, not shadows, to live free and not as a slave. She knew that the same one who had bent down to her hunger for the truth desires to fill that hunger in every mind and heart regardless of how weak or inadequate: "And who am I that you give me your truth? ...Your truth...does and accomplishes all things, because I am not. It is your truth that offers truth, and with your truth I speak the truth."[52]

Catherine once asked a friend to pray for her, "that God will give me grace ever to love and to proclaim the truth, and that for that truth I may die."[53] For the truth Catherine did die; but even more, for the truth, the living person of Jesus, she lived. As she reflected on the words of Scripture, "Put on the Lord Jesus Christ" (Rom 13:14), she began to see with Paul that Jesus himself is the truth that clothes us. And Jesus himself opened her to the depths of the Trinity, abyss of sincerity and truth: "O immeasurable love! O gentle love!... You are that fire ever blazing, O high eternal Trinity! You are direct without any twisting, genuine without any duplicity, open without any pretense."[54]

Clothed in the "garment who clothes us and pastures our starving with his sweetness," Catherine lived her life in the saving truth and so knew its freedom. She invites those who

---

[51]D 167, p. 367.

[52]Pr 21, p. 193.

[53]Let T 277 to Monna Alessa Saracini; Scudder, p. 271. This young aristocratic widow of Siena was Catherine's confidante and constant companion. Also a member of the *mantellate,* Alessa had a home near Catherine's to which the saint would frequently go for rest and refreshment, sometimes for weeks.

[54]Pr 9, p. 69.

find themselves "mirrored here" to taste this same radical freedom that truth gives, to love and to live the truth in their own lives. For herself and for all who find within themselves a thirst for truth, Catherine prays the prayer with which she ends her *Dialogue:* "Clothe, clothe me with yourself, Eternal Truth."[55]

[55]D 167, p. 377.

4

The Inner Dwelling

Catherine's insight into the power and beauty of living clothed in the truth led her to reflect on the path that leads to truth. Is it a difficult way reserved for a chosen few and beyond the reach of ordinary people, or is it a path open and possible even to those weighed down with activity and responsibility? From her own experience Catherine found the answer in Deut 30:11-14: the path "is not too hard for you, neither is it far off. . . The word is very near you. . .; it is in your heart." The Latin text of Lk 17:21 further opened to her the deep and simple way to truth: "The kingdom of God is within you."

Catherine shared with countless other mystics an attraction to this mystery of God within us, yet she sounded its depths and implications in a way marked with special relevance for us. Having desired in her youth to live totally absorbed in God as a hermit, Catherine discovered that the Holy Spirit would lead her to the truth not within the walls of a material hermitage but within the inner dwelling of her heart. In the midst of the extraordinary activity and public ministry to which God called her, the Holy Spirit taught her to bear within her an inner dwelling which she would never have to leave. As she grew faithful to living within her own heart, she found the dimensions of this inner cell expanding until they assumed the proportions of the lavish garden and lightsome home of God himself. Drawn by God's love within her, she learned to let the fire and warmth of this inner dwelling draw her simultaneously into God's embrace and outward into the arms of her brothers and sisters.

The Kingdom of God Within: The Cell of Self-Knowledge

Catherine was still young when she learned the importance of living continually in the cell of her heart. At an age when she should have been preparing herself for an eligible suitor, she alienated her family by refusing to consider even the prospect of marriage; her only spouse would be Jesus. To break her will, her family deprived her of any place or time which she could devote to prayer. But Catherine found a way to turn this obstacle into a blessing. The Holy Spirit inspired her to make a cell within her heart which she never had to leave, regardless of what she was doing.

In the past, she could spend time praying in the small room that she called her "cell" only when other responsibilities did not occupy her; but in this nonmaterial cell, she could stay always. For God's sake she had given up a physical cell made by human hands, and now God made for her a cell which no one could take from her. As Catherine explained to Raymond the value of her inner dwelling, he began to see that the inner cell comprises the reality of God's kingdom which we all can bear within us (Lk 17:21). And as Raymond himself became engrossed in his work and crushed under its burden, Catherine would remind him, "Build yourself a cell within your heart, and never put a foot outside it."[1]

---

[1] R 1.4, p. 47.

Catherine grew to understand that we discover truth finally in the fiber of our own experience, and that the depth of our own life forms the holy "place" where God calls us to live. But for Catherine, this implies no inner world of merely subjective truth, for she saw that God's engagement with us reveals the reality of God's identity and ours: the great goodness and love of God, and our own weakness and poverty without him: in this double truth Catherine began to find every blessing. She began to realize, too, that its treasure is utterly near to anyone who desires it, for the kingdom of God is within each one of us (Lk 17:21).

When we live not simply in hectic activity in the world outside us but also in deep engagement with the world within us, we begin to find a dwelling place within ourselves, a "holy abyss" where we come to know both God and ourselves.[2] Holy abyss: the words themselves indicate why Catherine loved to call the realization of who we are and who God is, a *cell.* The small, unadorned place where one prays is a cell. Hermits have cells in the crevices of rocks, in deserted and empty places where simplicity and silence allow their hearts to hear the gentle silence of God's heart. Catherine herself had set aside such a place in her own home, free from the noise and bustle of her large family.

But the word *cell* signifies for Catherine far more than this small place. When she first began to live within her heart, this inner dwelling served as a haven and escape from the real world around her. But with time, its small confines assumed increasingly spacious proportions and transparent dimensions. The inner cell became no longer a place of hiding but the lavish home of God whose generous love drew her both inward to his love and inseparably outward to her brothers and sisters.

As Catherine reflected on what "Truth itself" had taught her, that she should "know herself and God's goodness *at work* in her,"[3] she began to see that the inner cell indicates

---

[2]Let T 30 (DT 1) to the Abbess and Suora Niccolosa of the Monastery of Santa Marta in Siena.

[3]D 19, p. 57.

the dynamic activity of God taking place continually in our lives. The uncluttered space of a cell opens us to the depth of God's engagement with us at every second. And if we did not live superficially, our awareness of God's presence would flow into the time of day not spent in the material cell. Such awareness would cease to be an experience reserved for a few quiet moments in a place set apart; the material cell would increasingly become also the cell of our hearts, the inner home we would never have to leave. Precisely because our own lives are the "inner cell" where God's continual and intimate activity takes place, the Father tells Catherine, "Never leave the knowledge of yourself."[4]

"You Are the One Who Is Not: I Am the One Who Is"

Raymond describes how Catherine's spirituality stemmed from her initial experience of the inner cell, and how it unfolded around the one principal word which the Lord had spoken to her at the outset of her young adulthood. "Do you know, daughter, who you are and who I am? If you know these two things you have beatitude in your grasp. You are she who is not, and I AM WHO IS." Catherine felt the Lord promise her that she would find every possible blessing in this truth if she would let it fill her entire being.[5]

As Catherine shared this insight with Raymond, he saw how this word's deceptive brevity contains the entire treasure of life in the Spirit.[6] Experience shows us that we can do nothing apart from the Lord (Jn 15:5) and that, of ourselves, we "are not;" for by our own sin we often choose again the nothingness out of which God's love has drawn us. But with Paul we gradually learn to glory in the weakness which draws the power of Christ to us (2 Cor 12:9), and to yield our

[4]D 4, p. 29.
[5]R 1.10, p. 85.
[6]R 1.10, p. 86.

being to the God who lavishes upon us our life and every blessing as the sheer gift of love. We then begin to grasp with Paul the meaning of 2 Cor 6:20: "You are not your own; you have been bought with a price. So glorify God in your body."

"I am the One who is." Raymond found in this second part of the Lord's word to Catherine the entire treasure of the Hebrew and Christian scriptures, for all that we are and have comes from the God who loved us before we were, and whose love has created us worthy of love. We ourselves, along with all of creation, draw our life and being not simply once, in a moment, but at every second from the fullness of the God revealed to Moses as the One Who Is (Ex 3:14). The Father taught Catherine to let the beauty and power of this truth fill her mind and heart: "Learn to know, in your inmost heart, that I am in the most literal sense your Creator; and so you will have beatitude in your grasp."[7]

Two Inseparable Cells

Catherine began to understand that the inner dwelling comprises in fact two inseparable cells containing the knowledge of ourselves and of God's goodness: "You will know me in yourself, and from this knowledge you will draw all that you need."[8] In prayer Catherine saw how knowing ourselves draws us to love God,[9] for within our own lives we discover the height and depth, the length and breadth of God's goodness. As we become unafraid of our own need, we begin to discover within ourselves not a pit of emptiness but the very abyss of God.

This is why the experience of our weakness becomes God's own gift to us, since in realizing our poverty we come

[7]R 1 19, p. 88.
[8]D 4, p. 29.
[9]Let T 362 to Giovanna, Queen of Naples.

to know God's infinite goodness to us.[10] Rather than unfolding to us a self-knowledge filled with despair, the inner cell in this way opens us to the truth of our strength and beauty in God. Those who find this treasure are able to cry out with Mary and with all of God's poor ones: the Lord has "looked upon his lowly handmaid..., from this day forward, all generations will call me blessed" (Lk 1:47-48). Yet we can never know this wealth if we live superficially, outside the inner cell of self-knowledge: "I don't think it is possible to have virtue or the fullness of grace without dwelling within the cell of our heart and soul, where we will find the treasure that is life for us..., the holy abyss [of]...knowledge of ourselves and of God."[11]

Catherine found that if we try to live in only one of the cells, we will end either in despair or presumption. Knowing ourselves outside of God gives us nothing but confusion and discouragement at our own weakness, while knowing God's goodness without awareness of our own need opens us to pride and presumption.[12] In her counsel to others, Catherine stresses that knowing ourselves without knowing God gives us only part of the truth, for without any deeper reality in which to ground our self-knowledge, our own poverty becomes the final word about ourselves. This kind of self-knowledge ends in destroying the very self we sought to know. But when God's love and mercy form the heart of our self-knowledge, we live in the full truth of our beauty and goodness in God. Our own experience in this way teaches us the necessity of both cells.[13]

Each cell holds out its own blessings to us. In knowing ourselves we become humble and compassionate, and in knowing God we grow in love and charity. Catherine liked to picture the apostles as they shut themselves in the upper

[10]D 7, p. 36.

[11]Let T 30 (DT 1) to the Abbess and Suora Niccolosa of the Monastery of Santa Marta in Siena; Noffke, trans.

[12]Let T 49 to Monna Alessa dei Saracini and others; and Let T 23 to Nanna di Benincasa, Catherine's niece.

[13]Let T 51 to Frate Felice da Massa, Augustinian.

room to await the Spirit's outpouring. In this image of peaceful waiting she found a symbol of our own need to dwell within both inner cells, for in this way we gain the humility and charity which only the Spirit of love can form within us.[14]

Although both cells are inseparable, one of them becomes so essential that it contains and gives life to the other. Catherine thought of a blazing fire whose sparks, before falling to the ground, seem to shoot upward as if drawn back to their source. God's love is this fire for Catherine, we, the sparks; we have come from love and cannot help being drawn back to our source in God's love. And like the sparks that rise up to their source before they fall to the ground, we need to dwell in the cell of self-knowledge only as it is embraced by the cell of knowing God's infinite love and mercy: "Let's come down to know our own poverty and indifference, but only after we have gone upward.... There, when we find ourselves in the abyss of his charity—there will we be made humble!"[15]

God at the Heart of Darkness

When we begin to live in the inner dwelling, we soon enough encounter the time of trial, for we enter into our own depths where disorder and weakness dwell side by side with beauty and goodness. But we can escape this encounter with ourselves only at the price of losing ourselves and the treasure of God in ourselves. Raymond recounts how Catherine herself faced the struggle of the inner cell. Toward the end of her three-year period of seclusion, when she was about twenty, she found that she could barely think a thought of God or feel any love toward God. The path of ease and self-indulgence grew attractive to her, and temptations to impurity plagued her; her own life and quest for God

---

[14]Let T 94 to Frate Matteo di Francesco Tolomei, O.P.

[15]Let T 70 (DT 21) to Frate Bartolomeo Dominici, O.P.; Noffke, trans.

appeared as impossible as persevering in God's call. Yet even as she was tempted to despair, she would not give up praying, but would repeat what often seemed like hollow words, "I rely on the Lord Jesus Christ, and not upon myself."[16]

After a long period of these trials, Catherine seemed to experience one day a new light from the Holy Spirit. She began to understand that this struggle was in fact an answer to her own prayer for the gift of faith and courage, and she resolved to stand steadfast in it for as long as the Lord desired. In the light of this new understanding, the Lord made his presence known to her. Catherine begged him to tell her why he had abandoned her: "Where were you, Lord, while my heart was suffering the agony of all those horrors?" When the Lord answered that he had been present in her heart the entire time, she asked him how this could be, since her heart had been filled with "obscene and abominable thoughts." Jesus asked her who had kept her faithful and caused her to feel grief rather than delight at these temptations: "Was it not I myself, hidden in your heart's core?... It was I who was working in you all this time. Hidden in your heart, I was guarding it from your enemies on every side."[17]

This experience so impressed itself upon Catherine that she would later encourage others with the truth she had learned during this time. She realized that even when we love God, we often grow "not only lukewarm but altogether cold." Discouraged at feeling no love for God, we often give up prayer entirely and in this way only weaken ourselves still more.[18] But Catherine herself learned that we most need to pray when we least feel like praying, because the time of trial greatly increases our self-knowledge and dependence on God. "This knowledge is more perfectly gained in time of temptation, because then you know that you are nothing, since you have no power to relieve yourself of sufferings and troubles you would like to escape."[19]

[16]R 1.11, p. 98.

[17]R 1.11, pp. 101-02.

[18]R 1.11, pp. 99-100.

[19]D 43, p. 88.

We cannot flee the distractions and temptations that are part of the human condition, for our mind is often "beset by...perverse cogitations, so that it seems unable to think of God, and can hardly remember his name."[20] But the Lord permits us these struggles only so that we will recognize our weakness, and trust all the more in his power and mercy. Catherine reminds her friend Daniella that the devil tempts us only to make us despair, but the Lord allows us temptation only to increase our trust and surrender to him. *This* is the truth that must sustain us when we are discouraged; for, even when we do not surrender to sin, we often give in to an accompanying discouragement that tempts us to think, "You are no good because of the thoughts and impulses that fill you."[21] Not conquering in this first battle which tempts us to a specific sin, evil often overcomes us in this second one by seducing us into despair. For this reason, Catherine would remind her friends that the time of trial is God's own gift: "The wise soul, seeing that from this experience proceeds such profit, reassures itself...and will hold this time dearer than any other."[22]

As we recognize how adversity increases our desire for the very virtue we are struggling to gain, we learn by experience how God gives us in bitter things only sweetness, and reveals himself to us "at the heart of darkness."[23] God seems to be absent to us in the time of trial, and yet he is never closer to us than when we are enduring these struggles. Catherine would think of Jesus on the cross and how abandoned he felt even as the Father was utterly near to him. For our good, Jesus does the same with us, often withdrawing the feeling of his intimacy but never its reality.[24]

[20] Let T 227 to William Flete; Scudder, pp. 160-61.

[21] Let T 221 to Suor Bartolomea della Seta, nun of the monastery of Santo Stefano in Pisa; Scudder, p. 163.

[22] Ibid.

[23] Let T 189 (DT 84) to the monks of the Monastery of San Girolamo at Cervaia; and to Giovanni di Bindo, Niccolò di Ghida, and other monks of Monteoliveto Maggiore.

[24] Let T 221 to Suor Bartolomea della Seta.

God's Power Made Perfect in Weakness

Catherine realized that hardship tempts us to avoid the inner dwelling and in this way seduces us into pride and self-reliance.[25] Yet in our hearts we know how truly weak we are, and how we succumb at the slightest temptation.[26] But if we would cast ourselves on the Lord rather than relying on ourselves, we would find God in the depths of our own heart and experience for ourselves the truth of his words, "My grace is enough for you, for my power is made perfect in weakness" (2 Cor 12:9).

By staying faithful to the inner cell even in difficult times, we begin to discover the Holy Spirit within us, the Spirit whose power can change our grief into joy and peace.[27] Instead of escaping the inner cell when we feel weak and besieged, therefore, we must run to it as our refuge,[28] preferring to dwell here with struggle rather than anywhere else with apparent peace.[29] Catherine herself had found that the self-knowledge we gain here, though painful at first, heals us of self-reliance[30] and gives us in combat the rose of "perfect purity."[31]

Catherine's understanding of the purpose of temptation carries the mark of her own tenderness: God's goodness has devised a gentle paradox, so that every virtue is won only out of its contrary. Catherine saw temptation as God's means of strengthening us rather than weakening us, for if we never had to endure struggle, we would have in the place

---

[25]Let T 202 to Iacomo, doctor of medicine at Ascania; and Let T 197 to Matteo di Tommuccio da Orvieto.

[26]Let T 242 to Angelo da Ricasoli, bishop of Florence.

[27]Let T 211 (DT 70) to Raymond of Capua.

[28]Let T 76 to Frate Giovanni di Bindo of Monteoliveto Maggiore.

[29]Let T 36 to certain novices of Santa Maria di Monteoliveto.

[30]Let T 137 (DT 45) to Matteo Cenni, rector of the House of the Misericordia. Catherine here stresses trust in God's mercy as it enlarges our hearts precisely with the kind of compassion Matteo himself showed to the sick and poor.

[31]Let T 140 (DT 30) to John Hawkwood, at his camp.

of true virtue only the pretense of virtue. She saw that our desire for good increases immeasurably when we struggle with its opposite: "How is purity tested and won? Through the contrary.... Everything is driven out by its opposite. See how humility is won through pride."[32]

The Church liturgy for the Easter vigil cries out, "O happy fault that merited such a Redeemer!" As Catherine reflected on these words, she realized that the Lord can turn even our sin into the blessing of humility, charity, and increased dependence on him.[33] In the time of combat we know our helplessness and learn by experience not to rely on our own strength, since we "cannot hope in nothingness."[34] Our inability to end our own struggles makes us turn all the more willingly to the Lord, therefore, and to open our hearts to his power which alone can heal us.[35]

Because every sin masks a self-reliance that eats away our trust in God,[36] Catherine stresses that we arrive at the "harbor of perfection" only through the trials that force us to depend on God rather than on ourselves. She pictures the Lord's tenderness preserving us in the midst of our weakness, so that our falls serve only to humble us rather than to destroy us.[37] The time of trial should comfort rather than grieve us, therefore, because we travel the road that leads to God. "At no time does the soul know herself so well, if I am within her, as when she is most beleaguered."[38] Knowing ourselves in turn makes us know God's goodness and fidelity to us even in our weakness, as well as the beauty of the giver in the midst of the gifts he bestows: "I want them to want *me*."[39]

[32]Let T 211 (DT 70) to Raymond of Capua, in Avignon; Scudder, p. 135.

[33]Let T 219 (DT 65) to Raymond of Capua and others of his company, at Avignon.

[34]Let T 78 to Niccolò Povero, hermit at Florence.

[35]D 90, p. 168.

[36]Let T 211 (DT 70) to Raymond of Capua.

[37]Let T 83 to Conte di Conti, widely known for his assistance to poor prisoners.

[38]D 90, p. 168.

[39]D 49, p. 100.

Even the hardships we endure because of others bring us hidden blessings. Our humility is "tested by the proud," our faith by those without faith, our hope by the hopeless, our compassion by the cruel, our "gentleness and kindness by the wrathful." "Your neighbors are the channel through which all your virtues are tested and come to birth."[40] By staying faithful to the inner cell through interior and exterior struggles, we thus gradually grow in surrender to God, and experience for ourselves the truth that out of darkness, light is born; out of weakness, strength; and out of its contrary, perfection is won.[41]

You Will Find Yourself in God and God in Yourself

Catherine's own experience taught her that living in the inner cell gives us an appreciation not simply of our need, but especially of our value. "Never leave the knowledge of yourself," the Father tells Catherine, "for you will know me in yourself, and from this knowledge you will draw all that you need."[42] Our knowledge of God in this way becomes a "gentle mirror" in which we see both God's beauty and our own. For if we try to know ourselves outside of God, we see only a distorted image of ourselves; but if we see ourselves in the mirror of God's love we begin to recognize and to believe our own goodness in God whose love has made us worthy of love.[43]

"You will find yourself in him, and you will find him in yourself. . .and you will find in you the infinite goodness of God."[44] Catherine began to see that only by knowing God do we know ourselves as we really are, infinitely loved and

[40]D 8, pp. 38-39.

[41]Let T 211 (DT 70) to Raymond of Capua.

[42]D 4, p. 29.

[43]D 13, p. 48.

[44]Let T 226 to Raymond of Capua.

embraced by faithful love;[45] for we find the very reality of God within us: "Eternal Father, those who look at themselves find you within themselves. For they are created in your image. . . You are in us and we are in you."[46] And the more we live within the inner cell, the more we discover God's love burning brightly not only within us but all around us: "O fire ever blazing! The soul who comes to know herself in you finds your greatness wherever she turns, even in the tiniest things, in people and in all created things."[47] As we increasingly recognize God's goodness within our own lives,[48] we learn to praise God who formed our inward parts, knitting us together in our mother's womb. With the psalmist, we not only celebrate God's glory, "You are wonderful," but also cry out in praise, "I am wonderful" (Ps 139:13-14)!

Catherine writes to a friend that we should enter the inner dwelling the way we enter our own rooms when we are tired. Wanting only sleep, we do not linger at the door but go straight to bed. We who come to the inner cell must do the same; we are not to stop at the door of our weakness but run to the bed of God's mercy within our hearts.[49] Like the one who sees her image in a fountain, we who live in the inner cell must see not simply our defects but, beyond them, the image of our beauty in the fountain of God's love. We are then drawn to fall in love not with the image, but with the beauty of the fountain.[50]

Catherine liked to picture the inner dwelling as a well of clear water under the muddy earth. The earth is our misery, but deeper than this surges the clear water of God's love. "So let us enter into the depths of that well. . .and dwell *there*."[51]

---

[45]D 31, p. 73.

[46]Pr 22, p. 197.

[47]Pr 12, p. 100.

[48]Let T 185 (DT 54) to Pope Gregory XI, at Avignon.

[49]Let T 73 to Suora Costanza of the Monastery of Santa Abundio near Siena; Catherine considered this monastery a blessed place of God.

[50]Let T 226 to Raymond of Capua.

[51]Let T 41 (DT 3) to Frate Tommaso dalla Fonte, O.P.; Noffke, trans.

In another particularly gentle image she compares the dwelling of self-knowledge to the sepulcher which held the Lord. Magdalen was unable to push away the rock by herself; but as soon as she acknowledged her weakness, the huge stone was no longer an obstacle, and the Lord himself was present to her. Like the immense rock, our sin weighs heavily upon us, yet if we wait trustfully in the "sepulcher of self-knowledge," the burden of our sin recedes and we find Christ himself risen and radiant within us.[52]

The Blessings of the Inner Cell

The gifts of the inner cell increasingly drew Catherine to its mystery, for she found that here we discover joy, peace, and the continual prayer which keeps us wordlessly attentive to God in the midst of even hectic activity.[53] As we find God within us, we see also the depth of God's desire for us.[54] For God who is sheer love wants nothing but love from us,[55] a love we gain precisely in knowing ourselves and his mercy. When we see our absolute need for God and recognize that our life and every blessing come from God's tender mercy to us, our own hearts are inspired to return love for love: "Then we discover so much of God's goodness poured out on us that words cannot describe it. And once we see ourselves so loved by God, we cannot help loving him. And within ourselves we love God."[56]

[52]Let T 173 to a religious who left his order.

[53]Let T 334 to Cardinal Bonaventura of Padua, who, after his defense of Urban VI, was assassinated in 1379 at the instigation of a member of his own family.

[54]Let T 353 to Monna Catella, Cecia, and Caterina Dentice.

[55]Let T 145 (DT 40) to Queen Elizabeth of Hungary, mother of King Louis. The queen's devotion to Urban inspired her to send him a precious tierra in place of the one taken by French cardinals as they left Rome.

[56]Let T 241 (DT 73) to Monna Giovanna di Corrado Maconi, in Siena; Noffke, trans. Catherine's letter to the mother of her beloved friend and secretary, Stefano Maconi, stresses the peace and attachment to God's will that would not resent (as Giovanna did) her son's frequent absence from her.

But the dwelling of self-knowledge causes us to grow in love not only for God but also for one another, for as we know ourselves in God, the Spirit's own charity frees us for a generous and unpossessive love.[57] Catherine pictures the inner dwelling as warmed by the gentle fire of God's love; in the kindly light of this fire we see our own weakness and God's goodness. And as the fire's own warmth begins to take hold of us, the bitterness in our lives begins to be sweet, the weakness becomes strong, and "all the ice of selfish love melts away." Thus healed of selfishness, we learn to love generously. The paradox of the inner dwelling then reveals itself to us: in its warmth and inwardness we gain the love to reach out of ourselves, just as God's love does, to our brothers and sisters and to make their needs our own. "We pour out a river of tears and spread our loving desires out over all our sisters and brothers, loving them with a pure love, without self-interest."[58]

Reflecting on the apostles' encounter with the Holy Spirit after they had shut themselves in the upper room, Catherine invites her friends to expect and to desire this same lavish outpouring of the Spirit in their own lives.[59] "In the knowledge of yourself, you will find the sweet clemency of the Holy Spirit, who is given all entire, and who is nothing other than love." Deeper than our own weakness, then, we discover the very reality of God within us: "In the cell of your soul you will find God all entire, who gives such sweetness, peace, and consolation that nothing can trouble it, because it is filled with the will of God."[60]

Toward the end of her life Catherine wrote to Raymond, "You will be able to have the actual cell little; but I wish you to have the cell of the heart always, and always carry it with you."[61] This is the dwelling we can take wherever we go, the

---

[57]D 141, p. 292.

[58]Let T 141 (DT 38) to Don Giovanni de' Sabbatini of Bologna; Noffke, trans.

[59]Let T 351 to Pope Urban VI.

[60]Let T 241 (DT 73) to Monna Giovanna di Corrado Maconi.

[61]Let T 373 to Raymond of Capua; Scudder, p. 350.

place where our life lived in love becomes unceasing prayer.[62] "We will come" to you and "make our home" within you (Jn 14:23); far from being empty and barren, the inner cell blossoms as a garden full of beauty[63] and becomes the heaven and home which God our spouse never leaves.[64]

When we live continually within the inner dwelling we thus discover heaven on earth[65] and, tasting the great mercy of God in our lives, we begin to cry out gratefully with Catherine's own prayer: "No matter where I turn, I find nothing but your deep burning charity." Can we ever "repay the graces and burning charity" of God toward us? Catherine herself responds with the intimate knowledge she gained by never leaving the inner dwelling: "Only you, most gentle loving father, only you can be my acknowledgement and my thanks. The affection of your very own charity will offer you thanks, for I am she who is not."[66]

In a charming closing image Catherine pictures us so allured by the inner dwelling's beauty that once and for all we pull up stakes, pack our belongings and transfer all that we are and have into this cell, our true home. Once moved in, we will never want to leave. As Catherine had invited her own friends to live in this most wonderful of homes, she surely extends the same invitation now to us: "Let's not put off any longer our move into this holy dwelling of self-knowledge. We so need this, and it is so pleasant for us because...God's boundless goodness is there."[67]

---

[62]Let T 37 to Niccolò di Ghida. Catherine here invites the famous doctor to find the Lord's peace and presence in the midst of his demanding medical responsibilities, advice which his reputation for holiness shows that he heeded.

[63]Let T 241 (DT 73) to Monna Giovanna di Corrado Maconi.

[64]Let T 41 (DT 3) to Frate Tommaso dalla Fonte, O.P.

[65]Let T 215 to certain monasteries of Bologna.

[66]D 134, p. 273.

[67]Let T 141 (DT 38) to Don Giovanni de' Sabbatini of Bologna; Noffke, trans.

5

Our Mother Prayer

One especially familiar and tender image drew Catherine to discover within the inner dwelling, not only her own meaning, but also the meaning of prayer. As her ministry and travels placed her constantly in family settings, she was deeply touched by the intimate bond she saw between mothers and their nursing children. The infant's total helplessness and the mother's absolute presence to her child's need: in this unparalleled affection and closeness Catherine recognized the heart of God's communion with us. In prayer we find our mother. For just as a mother nourishes her child with her own milk, prayer feeds us with God's own nearness.[1] And this mother is unacquainted with the sorrow of bringing forth a dead child; for, as Catherine herself learned, rather than providing an escape from the world, prayer conceives and gives birth to a love not only for God but also for one another, a love alive with zeal for the world's healing.[2]

---

[1]Let T 245 to a Genoese man of the third order of St. Francis.

[2]Let T 26 to Suora Eugenia, Catherine's niece at the Monastery of Santa Agnesa di Montepulciano. Eugenia and her sister were daughters of Catherine's brother, Bartolo, and were both received into the monastery of Santa Agnesa. Eugenia is thought to have died while still a young sister, since her name does not appear on the community list at the chapter of 1387.

"Ask and It Will Be Given You"

As we read of Catherine's life we may be tempted to
equate her prayer with unbroken ecstasy and invisible stigmata, with visions and phenomena far removed from our
own experience. In reality, however, the prayer she learned
was as simple and available as a mother's closeness to her
infant's need. "Ask and it will be given you" (Lk 11:9); in the
inner cell Catherine discovered our own human need as the
heart of all prayer. The tenuousness of our relationships,
beautiful in their gift yet vulnerable to rejection and death;
the frailty of our accomplishments and successes, full of joy
yet able to be reversed or quickly forgotten: these and countless other experiences confront us with both our wealth and
our want. No one of us has to be; we are, in Catherine's
words, the "ones who are not." Yet rather than enslaving us
to worthlessness, our very need frees us to be who we really
are, the sheer gift of God's love.

Early in her life, Catherine discovered the significance of
the desire that springs from our need. As Raymond grew to
know Catherine, he saw how the central gifts of her life and
ministry flowed from the longing which God had first placed
within her. When her family had tried to prevent her from a
life of dedication to God in the world, she had begged the
Lord to grant her desire; but Raymond later realized that it
was in fact God's own desire within her that prompted her to
want what she did: "She asks that very thing which he himself who is sought for has invited us to seek. It is an asking
which cannot be in vain. . . . It is a seeking which cannot end
in failure."[3]

Again, after her period of solitude, the Lord answered
Catherine's desire for faith with the very gift he wanted for
her, espousing her to himself in fidelity and love.[4] And when
she later desired to pray the psalms but had little success in
learning how to read through the tutelage of her companion,

[3] R 1.3, p. 36.
[4] R 1.12, p. 107.

Catherine asked the Lord to teach her himself. Raymond was astounded to find her prayer answered.[5] Experiences such as these taught Catherine the importance of desire in prayer, as the Lord himself had shown her; "I am telling you what I want you to do. Never relax your desire to ask for my help."[6]

The Lord places good desires within us precisely to deepen our capacity to receive the very gift he wants to grant us: "I give you whatever you need, for it is I who gave you the very hunger and voice with which you call to me."[7] Catherine began to understand that the God who gives infinitely more than we could imagine without our asking will all the more give what he inspires us to ask. God did not create the world with its indescribable beauty, nor give us our lives at our request; the Father did not send Jesus in response to our own plans. Untold and unasked-for blessings are ours. Since God lavishes on us what we could not even think to request, how much more will the Lord answer with overwhelming generosity the very desire he places within us: "Who makes us desire and ask. . .? Only He. Then, if He makes us ask it, it is a sign that He means to fulfill it, and give us what we seek."[8]

Yet what if we ask and God seems not to listen? Catherine herself saw that we sometimes ask only "with words," and not with "our whole heart," or perhaps we desire something destructive for ourselves. In not receiving what we want, therefore, we do gain what we truly desire. "When we do not have what we ask, we really have it. . . God satisfies our intention. . . On God's side we always have our prayer."[9] This had been Augustine's experience: Monica's desire for her son's conversion prompted her to beg the Lord to prevent Augustine from going to Milan, since she feared that he

---

[5] R 1.11, p, 105.

[6] D 107, p. 201

[7] *Ibid.*

[8] Let T 258 to Ristoro Canigiani; Scudder, p. 201.

[9] Ibid.

would be further corrupted there. But in fact it was in this city that he would be converted. "In your deepest counsels," Augustine prays, "you heard the crux of her desire: You had no care for what she then sought, so that you might do for me what she forever sought."[10]

Sometimes, to "increase the hunger of our desire," the Lord waits to answer our prayer. Only after we have learned through the crucible of suffering to wait in patient trust and hope, depending on him and not on our own resources, does God grant our desire, and far more wonderfully than we could have imagined.[11] The gift we thus learn to want very much we are less likely to throw away once it is granted. This also was Augustine's experience; his conversion, because long-awaited, brought the fruit of peace and freedom all the more precious to his tortured soul. The very length of his suffering inspired his plea that the Lord prevent him from putting himself "up for sale again" after so great a gift.[12]

Sometimes God grants us the reality of what we ask without letting us feel that we have it: "He gives to us in effect though not in feeling." Our words and work may deeply touch others, yet we may feel useless and ineffective; or we may be filled with faith and charity even though we feel unbelieving and heartless. Catherine realized that the Lord permits us these feelings only to deepen our desire and capacity for the very gift we seek. At times, however, God answers our need by granting us both gift and feeling, and so we find that our desire is "always fulfilled."[13] And because the Lord wants to satisfy our every need,[14] the longing for good that he places within us, even when it is hesitant or only dimly recognized, both reflects and unites with the fire

[10]St. Augustine, *The Confessions* 5.8; in *The Confessions of St. Augustine,* translated, with introduction and notes by John K. Ryan (Garden City: Image Doubleday, 1960), pp. 123-24.

[11]Let T 258 to Ristoro Canigiani; Scudder, p. 202.

[12]St. Augustine, *Confessions* 9.2; Ryan, p. 206.

[13]Let T 258 to Ristoro Canigiani; Scudder, p. 202.

[14]Let T 26 to Suora Eugenia.

of God's own desire for us.[15] We can trust, therefore, that the God who inspires this desire for him within us certainly intends to satisfy it.[16]

The Prayer of Words and of Silent Communion

Catherine found the beginning of all prayer in vocal prayer, communion with God in words. Our tongues and voices enable us to join with the psalmists' prayer, praising and speaking as friend and child to God, crying out in pain or anger, pleading or cajoling, singing with joy, interceding and begging with supplication. But Catherine stresses that our words have value only to the extent that they express our heart. Mouthing words simply to perform the task of "saying our prayers" accomplishes nothing, since the true purpose of prayer is to deepen our love.[17] What matters, then, is not our words but God's love; for we find the "expansiveness" of God's mercy, not in the words we say, but in the reality of God's presence to us: "While she says the words she should make an effort to concentrate on my love."[18]

What words should we use in praying? Catherine herself loved to pray the psalms and the Divine Office, and for this reason she learned to read. Her companions also at times captured in writing some of the prayers which spontaneously welled up from her heart and voice. Often these prayers express the sentiments of Scripture or the spirit of the liturgical feast or season; most of all, they spring from Catherine's own experience as a woman at the heart of the Church she loved and longed to see made new.

When urging Gregory's return to Rome, for example, she offers her whole being for this purpose: "I have one body,

[15]Let T 353 to Monna Catella, Cecia, and Caterina Dentice.

[16]D 197, p. 201.

[17]Let T 150 to Frate Francesco Tebaldi, Carthusian, on the isle of Gorgona.

[18]D 66, p. 124.

and to you I offer and return it."[19] During this time in Avignon away from her beloved friends she prays also for those the Lord has given her "to love with a special love."[20] And one of the most famous prayers attributed to Catherine stems from her time at Val d'Orcia in the fall of 1377: "O Holy Spirit, come into my heart, by your power draw it to yourself." She asks Jesus to guard her from all evil thoughts and to "warm and inflame" her with "his most gentle love that every suffering may seem light" to her. "My holy Father and my gentle Lord, help me in my every need. Christ love! Christ love!"[21]

Whether we use the words of Scripture, the Divine Office, or our own words, their role is to prepare us for the prayer of the heart which Catherine calls mental prayer.[22] By allowing our words and thoughts to bring us to a restful silence before the Lord, a silence in which we do not want to speak, we learn to yield to the gift of God's intimate presence. When we are drawn to this inner quiet, we need to let go of our words,[23] for if we continually ignore the Lord's "visitation" in order to complete our "tally of prayers," our prayer will never deepen.[24]

Catherine stresses the importance of not resisting when we feel drawn to this inner stillness, and of postponing our vocal prayer for a later time. But if lack of time prevents us from completing our "prayers" after this wordless union, we should not be disturbed, since the whole point of prayer is remaining in the Lord's healing presence rather than simply completing our own words and reflections.[25] Should we stop praying when we feel no inclination to this silent resting in God's presence? As Catherine herself learned, we most need

[19]Pr 1, p. 20.

[20]Pr 2, p. 26.

[21]Pr 6, p. 54

[22]Let T 150 to Frate Francesco Tebaldi.

[23]Let T 26 to Suora Eugenia, Catherine's niece.

[24]D 66, pp. 125-26.

[25]D 66, p. 124.

to pray when we least feel like praying. Even when we seem unable to pray as we ought, we can trust that the Spirit prays within us with "sighs too deep for words" (Rom 8:26), for the prayer of the heart depends not on our temperament or natural capacity for quiet but on the Spirit's presence and gift meant for each of us.

If we yield our mind and heart to the Lord's love rather than focusing simply on our words, we gradually become receptive to a prayer of inner quiet which rests in God's presence even as we pray with thoughts and words.[26] At times, we may taste the Lord's sweetness in prayer, and at other times remain wordlessly in the apparent dryness and emptiness which are in fact the Lord's nearness to us. Often, repeating a phrase from Scripture or one which wells up spontaneously from our heart will foster the inner quiet of prayer. We know that Catherine herself continually invoked the Lord's saving blood[27] and repeated phrases such as "Lord have mercy on me,"[28] "O God, come to our assistance! Lord, make haste to help us,"[29] and "Gentle Jesus, Jesus love."[30] As she learned to yield to this quiet resting in God, her vocal prayers gradually decreased until she could barely finish the words of an Our Father.[31]

Difficulties in Prayer

Having begun enthusiastically to give ourselves to God's love, we soon enough find, as Catherine herself did, that our good feelings give way to coldness and indifference. The path of prayer in this way leads us where we would least expect. But the Lord wants to expand our heart with hope in

[26] *Ibid.*
[27] Pr 8, p. 65.
[28] Pr 14, p. 124.
[29] Pr 15, p. 136.
[30] Pr 5, p. 49.
[31] R 1.11, p. 105.

his mercy and power even when we feel nothing but emptiness and discouragement.[32] Catherine stresses the importance of staying faithful to prayer precisely when we are
tempted to abandon it, if we want to know true intimacy
with God.[33] We naturally cling to the gift rather than to the
giver; and yet, when we cannot think a holy thought or feel
any love, God himself weans us away from a selfishness
masked as spirituality. As Catherine herself learned, far
from depriving us of God's presence, dryness and emptiness
in prayer bring us close to him because they force us to rely
not on our own thoughts and feelings but on God.[34] If we
respond with sadness and discouragement or quit prayer
altogether when we are deprived of consolation, we will
never grow beyond the mediocre.[35]

Catherine's ministry of counseling others taught her that,
rather than our weakness and sin, discouragement emerges
as our true enemy, pulling us from the arms of God's
mercy.[36] We feel abandoned by God when we suffer through
emptiness, distractions, and temptation; discouraged by our
struggles, we begin to lose interest in prayer and to think that
we are wasting our time. Yet because we "are not," abandoning prayer leads only to our own impoverishment. Only the
Lord can enlarge our heart, filling our life and ministry with
his power, and he often comes closest to us precisely when
we feel furthest from him.[37]

To friends enduring these trials in prayer, Catherine offers
the wisdom she herself had learned. Rather than discourag-
ing us, our inability to think a holy thought or to produce
the least act of love should prompt us to offer our weakness
to the Lord and to receive it again from his hands as a

---

[32]D 66, p. 124.

[33]R 1.11, pp. 99-100.

[34]D 63, p. 120.

[35]D 70, p. 132.

[36]Let T 169 to Frate Matteo Tolomei, O.P., and Don Niccolò, Carthusian.

[37]Let T 335 to Don Cristofano, Carthusian of the Monastery of San Martino in
Naples.

blessed friend. Instead of interpreting problems in prayer as a sign of God's absence, we thus gradually discover how truly God's ways teem with paradox, for we find death giving birth to life, and sorrow giving way to joy.[38]

In another letter Catherine focuses on the mistaken idea that revelations or pleasant feelings form the essence of true prayer. If we center our attention on good "experiences" in prayer, we build on sand, since consoling feelings and visions may come from a source other than God. Yet the Lord does give us consolation at times, only to draw us all the more surely to the giver rather than to the gift.[39] And when we grow attached to the comforts of prayer, the Lord gently leads us by the path of emptiness and darkness, of temptation and humiliation. Catherine encourages us to wait patiently and humbly in the emptiness rather than to abandon prayer, allowing God to anoint us during this time with the healing balm of faith and trust.[40] If we cling fast to our mother prayer even when we feel tempted to abandon her, the gentle "conflicts and shadows" of this mother will gradually show us that in our poverty the mercy of the "one who is" continually enfolds us.[41]

To another person Catherine writes that the temptations which accompany our growth in prayer should not frighten nor disturb us. Our body may revolt against the spirit and we may seem devoid of virtue, but God's mercy permits us humbling experiences only so that we will trust and depend on him alone. These struggles become the "very sweet wounds" meant to push us into the arms of God's mercy. Instead of abandoning prayer when we feel empty and attacked, we learn to take comfort in God's desire for intimacy with us, and to trust his providence in the very struggles which draw us to his mercy.[42]

[38] *Ibid.*

[39] Let T 340 to Monna Agnesa da Toscanella.

[40] *Ibid.*

[41] Let T 26 to Suora Eugenia; Scudder, p. 50.

[42] Let T 4 to a Carthusian monk in prison.

Catherine also stresses the importance of letting the Lord lead us in prayer rather than attaching ourselves to our own path or method. Having experienced God's visitation in one manner at a particular time, we may begin to seek God only through this path: "In her foolishness she looks for my gift only in that one way, trying as it were to impose rules on the Holy Spirit." But the Lord gives his presence in myriads of ways, and wishes us to receive him in the way he chooses and not in our own. Sometimes the Lord gives us a deep inner gladness; at other times, sorrow for sin; at still other times, an inner quiet. Yet the Lord acts within us, giving us what we most need, even when we feel nothing at all. God thus desires our attachment, not to feelings nor to a particular method of prayer, but to him so that we trust his love for us even when we do not feel it.[43]

Discernment of True Prayer

At times, the Lord does give us consolations and interior revelations in prayer. Yet how can we know if these are from God? In her advice for discerning God's visitation, Catherine stresses that God's gifts do not necessarily have the immediate result of good feelings, but they do have the long-term effect of growing in love and compassion. Gladness and desire for virtue accompany God's visitation, while "that which comes from the devil brings merely the gladness;" a close look shows that "there is not more virtue than there was before," since our delight comes only from love of our own consolation. When we are deluded in prayer, we cling to good feelings and visions without virtue; rather than fostering humility and charity, our experiences in prayer only feed our self-centeredness. But when we love God instead of our own satisfaction, we learn to love the gift because of the giver. When consolations pass and we are left again in emptiness and darkness, rather than rebelling, we give ourselves

---

[43]D 68, p. 129.

humbly to the God whose love we can trust even when we do not feel it.[44]

Catherine realized that the good feelings that come from love of our own consolation produce only momentary gladness and long-term "pain and pricking of conscience, without any desire for virtue." But the joy that comes from God anoints our heart with humility and sets it ablaze in the furnace of God's own charity and zeal.[45] For beautiful feelings and visions may be only delusions increasing our selfishness, while on the other hand, we may feel only darkness and emptiness and yet grow steadily in humble and zealous love. Catherine learned in this way to discern true prayer, not by our thoughts and feelings during prayer, but by the fruit that remains in our life after prayer.

Three Stages of Love

Her own call to love in the Church colored the way Catherine symbolizes our growth in closeness to God. She pictures the body of Jesus crucified as a bridge that binds heaven with earth, a bridge with three steps that ascend not simply as interior states relating us to God but also as degrees of love uniting us inseparably to others. In the early stages of prayer we still live in slavish fear, loving God and one another selfishly; like the sinful woman, we cling initially only to the first stair, the feet of Jesus. At the second stair, however, we come to the Lord's side and learn to love God and others unselfishly, as friends. At the last stair we experience the intimate kiss of the Lord's mouth and find union not only with him but also with the whole of creation for whom Jesus has poured out his life.[46]

Catherine's passionate nature also drew her to picture different kinds of tears that accompany the stages of love.

[44]D 106, p. 200.

[45]D 106, p. 198.

[46]D 79, p. 148.

Before our conversion to the Lord, we know "bitter tears" that flow when worldly and sinful experiences fail us. These "wretched tears" and "tormented weeping" well up from our grief when we find ourselves betrayed by the very people and pleasures we had trusted.[47] The first stages of prayer thus bring us to healing tears of sorrow and repentance, and eventually to heartfelt gratitude for the Lord's mercy to us. Yet because of the "agreeableness of the consolation" and delight we find in God, our love is "tender" but not strong.[48] In the later stages of prayer, however, we weep tears that flow from a will made perfectly one with God; no longer desiring anything except what God wants, we find ourselves "clothed" in a charity that weeps when God is offended and our "neighbors hurt."[49]

Prayer in this way gives birth to a love that draws us into God's own heart, where we learn to labor and pray for the world's *yes* to God's mercy. The Father asks Catherine to unite herself to Jesus' own intercession precisely because intimacy with him gives us this "fragrance" of a heart on fire with zeal: "Through your weeping and constant humble prayer I want to be merciful to the world."[50]

Catherine began to realize that our tears of desire for the world's healing do not cease in heaven, for when we enter into its embrace, our tears of water become "tears of fire." The communion of saints swells as one chorus joined with the infinite power of Jesus' intercession: "The blessed come from their weeping to gladness. They receive everlasting life with the fruit of their tears and flaming charity: they cry out and offer tears of fire for you in my presence."[51]

Yet these tears of fire are possible to us even now; if we are unable to cry, if we long to weep physical tears for the world's healing and cannot, there is another way: "Likewise

[47]D 90, p. 166; D 94, p. 175.
[48]D 95, p. 177.
[49]D 90, p. 167.
[50]D 166, p. 363.
[51]D 96, p. 182.

the Spirit helps us in our weakness; for we do not know how to pray as we ought, but the Spirit himself intercedes for us with sighs too deep for words" (Rom 8:26). Catherine pictures us weeping "with fire" when we are unable to cry, just as the Spirit weeps tears of fire instead of water for the world's salvation. "This is how the Holy Spirit weeps. Since the soul cannot do it with tears, she offers her desire to weep for love of me." The very person of the Spirit in this way "weeps" in us when we offer God the "fragrance of holy desire and constant humble prayer."[52]

Mystical Union

Raymond describes how Catherine gave herself, at the Lord's behest, to a life of ministry, but "did not diminish by one iota her life of intense and continual prayer." The more her love engaged her in service to others, the more this love became an interior fire that impelled her also to prayer.[53] Her prayer, in turn, pushed her to the heart of the world where the needs of her brothers and sisters became her own. She became convinced in this way that God calls to mystical union each one of us, no matter how weak and imperfect, if only we will surrender to this love: "You have drawn me to yourself in unutterable love, and you draw all of us to yourself not because you must but freely—if only we choose to let ourselves be drawn to you."[54]

In her writings, Catherine devotes little attention to describing interior states of prayer and union, and concentrates instead on God's goodness and our call to an intimacy with God that overflows in apostolic zeal. Yet when she does speak of mystical union, the Johannine writings often give her images to put into words what she knows words cannot contain: "What tongue could describe the marvel of this final

---

[52]D 91, p. 169.

[53]R 2.2, p. 120.

[54]Pr 1, p. 19.

unitive stage...perfect union—you cannot describe it with your tongue, which is a finite thing!"[55] The insight of Jn 14:21-23 offered Catherine a symbol of the intimate love at the heart of mystical union, a love which heals our selfishness and clothes us in God's own will: "If you will love me and keep my word, I will show myself to you, and you will be one thing with me and I with you."[56]

Catherine compares the purifying process that leads to mystical union to a coal thrown into a white-hot furnace. In the fire of God's charity we become like the burning coal, keeping "nothing at all, not a bit" of our own will outside of God because we are "set afire" with God's love.[57] The more we live "in God," the more the Spirit's love heals us of self-centeredness, so that the path which seemed so difficult to us at first becomes sweeter and more alluring with time.[58] "In the fire you fuse your will with hers and hers with yours." Rather than providing us with consoling experiences, mystical union clothes us in the radiance of God's own will and in "light, in fire, and in union," enchaining us with a love so strong that nothing can separate us from God.[59]

While we are still imperfect in love, God plays a "lover's game" with us, alternating his presence with seeming absence, teaching us to cling to the giver instead of the gift. But the reality of mystical union makes this game unnecessary, for love opens us to God's presence whenever we wish: "Every time and place is for them a time and place of prayer."[60] Catherine herself in this way experienced the truth of Jn 15:15: "Those who love me will be one with me and I with them, and I will show myself to them and we will make our dwelling place together."[61] God becomes the home we

---

[55] D 96, p. 181.

[56] D 1, p. 25.

[57] D 78, p. 147.

[58] Pr 25, p. 214; D 78, pp. 145-46.

[59] Pr 11, p. 93.

[60] D 78, p. 145.

[61] D 61, p. 116.

never have to leave; as water surrounds and embraces the fish, becoming its very life, we begin to live in God like the "fish in the sea and the sea in the fish," with our selfishness "drowned" in the love that enfolds us like a "peaceful sea."[62] And since "secrets are shared only with the friend who has become one with oneself," this mystical union brings us beyond a servant's love to that of a dear friend from whom God keeps no secret.[63]

Catherine's most intimate symbol for mystical union pictures a child resting in its parent's arms, filled with the peace given by the parent's kiss. Recalling the stages of love first at the Lord's feet, then at his side, and finally at his mouth, her image visualizes the tender union which makes us God's "very dear children," content to receive from his mouth the kiss of unbroken gladness and peace.[64] Here we feed on the milk of God's love "just as an infant when quieted rests on its mother's breast, takes her nipple, and drinks her milk through her flesh. This is how the soul who has reached this final stage rests on the breast of Christ crucified."[65] This closeness, the Lord tells Catherine, surpasses all the human heart could desire: "If anyone should ask me what this soul is, I would say: She is another me, made so by the union of love.... Not even the soul's own will stands between us, because she has become one thing with me."[66]

Because mystical union "inebriates" us with the blood of Jesus and inflames us with his love,[67] we experience an intimate bond not only with God, but also with God's children, our brothers and sisters. Catherine cannot conceive of a mystical union divorced from passion for the world's salvation, nor an intimacy with God that does not impel us to lavish upon others the gratuitous love we cannot return to

[62]Pr 2, p. 25.
[63]D 61, pp. 115-16.
[64]D 78, p. 147.
[65]D 96, p. 179.
[66]D 96, p. 181.
[67]D 79, p. 147.

God.[68] As we arrive at the third stair, that of the Lord's mouth, the place of perfect intimacy, our mouth begins to praise and to proclaim God; the "tongue" of our continual prayer speaks with the interior language of interceding for others and the external language of proclaiming the Word.[69] Our repose with the Lord in mystical prayer thus pushes us to the Church's very heart,[70] where we give ourselves through proclamation and intercession.[71]

The Fruit of Mystical Union: Intercession

"He is able for all time to save those who draw near to God through him, since he always lives to make intercession for them" (Heb 7:25). The Father awakened Catherine to the mystery of the Savior who continually prays for us, pouring out upon the world the same blood that has won our salvation. She realized in this way that mystical union calls us to intercede through "weeping and constant humble prayer" for God's mercy upon the world:[72] "I want you to pray to me for them so that I can be merciful to them."[73]

Catherine loved to reflect on the infinite value of a free human response to God: "Though you created us without our help, it is not your will to save us without our help."[74] But it is no easy thing for us to enter into this reciprocal bond of love with God, for selfishness and fear often raise barriers in us to the very love that could free and heal us. Catherine saw that when we use the "hand of free choice" to "encrust" our heart in resistance, only the blood of Jesus can give us love infinite enough to "shatter the diamond" of our

---

[68] Pr 11, p. 91.

[69] D 76, p. 140.

[70] Let T 150 to Frate Francesco Tebaldi, Carthusian.

[71] D 96, p. 181.

[72] D 166, p. 363.

[73] D 30, p. 71.

[74] D 134, p. 276.

obstinacy: "In spite of their hardness, let them...seek the blood of my Son and with that same hand...pour it over the hardness of their heart."[75] Only the blood of Jesus, continually poured out upon the world through his intercessory prayer, has the power to soften our resistance.

For this reason, Jesus' scars remain seared into his risen body as a living prayer crying out before the Father for us.[76] The blood flowing from these wounds makes the infinite love of God for us visible, and nothing so draws our free response as love: "Invite them, entice them, boundless love, so that they may be converted to you, my God."[77] Since love binds us to those we love, when we join ourselves to Jesus' intercession, we unite ourselves also to the ones for whom we intercede. In the power of Jesus' blood, our intercessory prayer in this way becomes a living *yes* within the hearts of those for whom we intercede; because of our union with them through love, our *yes* becomes in some sense their *yes* to the outpouring of God's mercy upon them. Catherine herself discovered that our prayer for those close to us has particular power before God because love forms the heart of intercession, and the Father himself places within us a "special" love for the ones he has given us.[78]

Catherine discovered, too, the consoling truth that the power of intercessory prayer does not depend on our own virtue. Her experience that "we are the ones who are not"[79] taught her to ask for God's own voice in crying out for mercy upon the world.[80] Those the Lord had "put on her shoulders" she learned to put back on his shoulders: "I give them back to you, since I am weak and inadequate."[81] Love thus focused her attention not on her own deficiencies but on

[75]D 4, p. 32.
[76]Pr 14, p. 118; Pr 9, p. 73.
[77]Pr 25, p. 217.
[78]Pr 2, pp. 26-27.
[79]D 134, p. 274.
[80]Pr 9, p. 73.
[81]Pr 14, p. 123.

the power of the God to whom intercessory love united her. She understood that since everything fails except in God, our own weakness and sin, far from obstructing the power of our intercessory prayer, all the more call down the divine mercy upon us and upon those for whom we pray:[82] "No matter where I turn I find nothing but your mercy. This is why I run crying to your mercy to have mercy on the world."[83] And because mercy is God's own identity, God's tenderness cannot resist giving it to whoever asks for it.[84]

When we ask for mercy upon the world, however, we intercede for nothing less than the outpouring of Jesus' blood upon it. Love teaches us to "knock at the door" of God's heart unceasingly, since what we seek is the "blood of this door." His blood is ours because God has made it a bath for us: "You neither can nor will refuse it to those who ask it of you in truth.... Open, then, unlock and shatter the hardened hearts of your creatures...and through this blood... be merciful to the world."[85]

Through her prayer, Catherine discovered intercession not as an optional devotion but as the Father's own invitation to each one who seeks intimate union with him: "Never lower your voice in crying out to me to be merciful to the world.... Through this...crying out it is my will to be merciful to the world."[86] Since the Father himself asks us to intercede for our brothers and sisters, we pray with the very prayer God places within us: "It is you who make them cry out: so listen to their voices.... I am asking you to grant what you are making me ask."[87]

Having discovered the inseparability of the two "wings of love," love for God and for one another,[88] Catherine began

[82]Pr 3, p. 38; Pr 2, p. 26.
[83]Pr 6, p. 69.
[84]D 134, p. 275.
[85]D 134, pp. 276, 275.
[86]D 107, p. 201.
[87]D 134, p. 275.
[88]R 2.1, p. 116.

to understand that mystical union of necessity flames forth in the generous service and intercession we owe as a debt of love to others.[89] Mystical union is reality for us only to the extent that we unite ourselves to one another through love and intercessory prayer: "The more you offer me...desires for them, the more you will prove your love for me."[90] The Father can heal the world without our intercession, yet Catherine realized that because of the very nature of love he has chosen to save us only with our free response. Mystical union thus joins us to God's own compassion, so that we can offer this same compassion to others;[91] the unselfish love we can never repay to God we can and must give to one another.

Catherine's experience gradually taught her that the power of intercessory prayer surpasses every work we might undertake for God's glory, since it joins our desire for the world's healing to the "fiery mercy of the Holy Spirit."[92] For this reason the Father invites us to feed the flame of our desire and to let "not a moment pass without crying out" for others.[93] And because intercession directs us in generous love to the needs of our brothers and sisters, the more we hunger for the world's salvation, the more we gain intimacy with the triune God: "The more they abandon themselves, the more they find me," the Father tells Catherine,[94] for mystical union joins us to God's own "hungry desire for the salvation of souls."[95]

Seeing that the Father's love drives him to answer even before we call,[96] Catherine grew increasingly bold in the prayer this love inspired in her: "I beg you—I would force

[89]D 6, p. 34.

[90]D 129, p. 255.

[91]Pr 15, p. 128.

[92]D 4, p. 29.

[93]D 4, p. 32.

[94]D 145, p. 304.

[95]D 8, p. 39.

[96]D 134, p. 276.

you even!—to have mercy on your creatures."[97] On feast days, especially of Mary, she would pray with even greater audacity: "Today I plead with you boldly because it is the day of graces, and I know, Mary, that he can deny you nothing."[98] Because she called out to him with the very love he placed in her heart, Catherine knew that the Father could not refuse opening to her the door of his "immeasurable charity." She would thus recall to him that he is glorified by people's conversions and not by "letting them stubbornly persist in their hardness." And since the Father has already created the entire universe out of nothing, she would remind him that converting even the most hardened sinner simply accomplishes the far more easy task of "remaking" what he has already made from nothing. All the more boldly, then, she prays, "Force their wills and dispose them to want what they do not want."[99]

Because they are anointed with the Holy Spirit and con-formed to Jesus' own heart, Catherine calls those who inter-cede "christs": "O best of remedy givers! Give us then these christs, who will live in continual watching and tears and prayers for the world's salvation."[100] The Father himself had invited Catherine and all those united with her to become "christs" for the Church, to draw their tears and intercessory prayer from the "fountain" of his love, and to use them to "wash the face" of his bride the Church: "Not by...violence will she regain her beauty but through peace and through the constant and humble prayers and sweat and tears poured out by my servants with eager desire."[101]

As she internalized these words of the Father to her, Catherine found that intercessory prayer increasingly be-came for her a joyful feast rather than a difficult task: "Because she is hungry she feasts on...charity for her

[97]D 13, p. 50.
[98]Pr 18, p. 164.
[99]D 34, p. 276.
[100]Pr 19, p. 179.
[101]D 16, p. 54.

neighbors."[102] She saw in prayer that heaven is filled with our blessed brothers and sisters who form one immense chorus of love and intercession for us.[103] Her own "banquet" of intercessory prayer became a pledge for her of heaven's gladness, a foretaste of the unbridled joy that charity alone effects.[104]

Ecstatic Union

Catherine's foretaste of heaven through intercessory prayer found a parallel in her experience of ecstasy. Raymond writes that the intensity of her love for God and others often caused this charity to break through into her body; when the thought of Jesus came to her mind, "her soul would withdraw as much as possible within herself, leaving her bodily senses."[105] Although reluctant to write of her own graces in prayer, Catherine sometimes does describe experiences which the reader recognizes as Catherine's. She reflects on the love that can take hold of a person and so unite her with God that the fire of charity begins to lift her beyond her body's narrow limits. When the force of love uniting her to God becomes stronger than the union between her soul and body, the power of this love breaks through even into her body.[106] God's love then draws to itself all of her powers, so absorbing the body's strength that the senses seem chained.[107]

At the heart of ecstasy is love so strong that it "lifts the body's weight off the ground, and the body is, as it were, immobile."[108] Because of the charity which inflames the

[102]D 101, p. 192.

[103]D 41, p. 84.

[104]D 101, p. 192.

[105]R 2.2, p. 120.

[106]D 142, p. 295.

[107]Let T 263 to Monna Montagna.

[108]D 79, p. 148.

soul's faculties, the body feels nothing: "The eye sees without seeing; the ear hears without hearing; the tongue speaks without speaking." But as Catherine herself experienced, the Lord sometimes allows a person in ecstasy to speak and thus to unburden her heart of its weight of joy and love. And while the body cannot bear the force of this union for long, the person's memory is "filled only with God" long after the ecstasy is over.[109]

Those who experience ecstasy may receive the gift of prophecy during it,[110] or perhaps they see into the hearts of those for whom they are praying, as Catherine herself did.[111] At other times, they may gain a deep but inarticulate knowledge of God's life and beauty.[112] Yet because of the limitations of our present life, all that they "see" now through mystical union is more like not seeing. And the gift of mystical prayer may be theirs side by side with a humbling "thorn in the flesh" which keeps their experience of the Trinity's heights grounded in the fertile soil of humility.[113]

Yet even with our weakness, ecstasy is meant to increase our desire for heaven; the power of love in ecstasy causes the body to cry out with all of its force for the perfect union of heaven. And if our body did not prevent us from constantly experiencing this union here on earth, we would literally die of love.[114] For those in heaven, however, the fire of ecstatic love is unceasing in its force: "I am to them a peaceful sea with which the soul becomes so united that her spirit knows no movement but in me."[115] In heaven's bliss, our desire for God is filled to overflowing; we know unending hunger without pain and satiety without boredom, because our

---

[109] *Ibid.*

[110] D 89, p. 166.

[111] Let T 233 (DT 76) to Pope Gregory XI.

[112] D 89, p. 166.

[113] D 83, p. 153.

[114] D 79, p. 148.

[115] D 79, p. 147.

every desire is immediately and perfectly filled with the immensity of God.[116]

Continual Prayer

"Pray at all times in the Spirit" (Eph 6:18). Catherine stresses that the continual prayer of the heart attentive to God in everything, rather than the experience of ecstasy, lies at the center of our mystical call. Just as vocal prayer leads us to wordless communion with God, contemplative prayer itself opens us to the continual prayer which Paul treasured: "Pray constantly " (1 Th 5:17). But how can we pray continually in the midst of the pressing responsibilities which occupy our mind and consume our energies? Catherine herself learned that rather than constituting an impossible ideal, continual prayer grows as the inevitable fruit of a heart that loves. Those who love know the experience of being preoccupied with responsibilities and yet having their hearts wordlessly directed to the beloved. As soon as their minds are free, their inner gaze turns spontaneously to the loved one. Parents bear their children within them even when they are not consciously adverting to their presence; this unconscious attention of the heart enables them to recognize immediately the cry of their own child even in the midst of loud noise.

In a similar way, "continual prayer" means "continual desire;" when we live in the Lord's presence we direct the desire of our heart to him in a wordless union deeper than our explicit thoughts, and in a way that underlies all that we do.[117] Catherine saw in this kind of prayer, not a luxury reserved to a contemplative few, but the indispensable condition of life itself. Unless we draw our energies from a source deeper than our own activity, our very responsibilities begin to consume and finally destroy us. The wordless prayer of

[116]D 79, p. 149.

[117]Let T 353 to Monna Catella, Cecia, and Caterina Dentice.

our heart in this way forms the wellspring from which we can draw our very life.

Catherine herself saw that continual prayer gives us a way to direct our heart to God even as pressing responsibilities engage our attention. When we pray "always," we devote ourselves to God through a desire and self-surrender deeper than our conscious thoughts. With this wordless prayer of the heart, we do not simply exist, we live; even in the midst of turmoil, a peace embraces us at the deepest level of our being, a peace which nothing can wrest from us (Jn 14:27).[118]

Continual Prayer as Love in Action

"Whatever you do in word or deed for the good of your neighbor is a real prayer;" from her own experience Catherine learned the identity of continual prayer and love ministering to others.[119] Yet for her, this does not mean simply that our work is our prayer; on the contrary, she stresses the absolute necessity of devoting time to explicit prayer. But Catherine's own call taught her the indispensable union between active and contemplative love, for she herself had learned that true ministry springs only from intimacy with God, while this intimacy in turn pushes us into the heart of the world.[120] Love communing with God and love ministering to others then become one same reality: "One who never stops doing good never stops praying."[121]

Without love "I am nothing" (1 Cor 13:2). The Lord had shown Catherine that if we seek our own consolation by refusing love to those in need, we cut ourselves off from the very God we seek in prayer. Since love alone is the heart and purpose of prayer, we corrupt the very meaning of prayer when we live selfishly. And because God's very being is love,

[118]Let T 4 to a Carthusian monk in prison.

[119]D 66, p. 127.

[120]D 66, p. 126.

[121]D 66, p. 127.

our refusal to help others diminishes our union not only with our brothers and sisters but also with God.[122]

Catherine would stress in her counsel to others the lesson she herself had learned, that we cannot love God if we do not love others. Because it comes from her own experience, her description of the selfish contemplative cannot help striking a chord in the heart of the reader. To live selfishly is to live under the illusion that our prayer unites us to God when in fact it does not. Instead of contemplative peace, agitation is ours. Since our heart is set not on God but on our own consolation, when we are forced to help another, we do so out of necessity rather than love. Catherine herself thus learned that prayer alone fosters love, but even a lifetime spent in prayer is useless to us if at death we are found without charity for one another.[123]

When she had invited certain hermits to join her at Rome in prayer and witness for the Church, the selfish refusal of her close friend William Flete prompted this stinging reply from Catherine: "Apparently God is an acceptor of places, and is found only in a wood, and not elsewhere in time of need."[124] For the sake of a deeper call to minister at Rome, she herself had sacrificed the solitude she desired after the Lord had seared this word into her heart: "Those who want to gain lose, and those who are willing to lose gain." Catherine understood the implications of this word to her: "Those who are willing to lose their own consolation for their neighbor's welfare receive and gain me and their neighbors, if they help and serve them lovingly. And so they enjoy the graciousness of my charity at all times."[125]

In his own summary of Catherine's prayer life, Raymond tells us how she had clung to prayer as her true mother and had "striven, with all she could command of zeal and perse-

---

[122]D 69, p. 131.

[123]D 69, p. 132.

[124]Let T 328 to Frate Antonio da Nizza; Scudder, pp. 314-315.

[125]D 69, p. 131.

verance, to acquire the habit of unremitting prayer."[126] This mother had fed and nourished her through consolation and temptation, had held her close to the breast of God, and had tenderly cared for her in her every need. It was this mother whose fidelity and nearness had inspired her lyrical hymn of praise to God for the gifts of prayer. Where are we healed of pride and selfishness, and where do we gain in their place a humble and generous heart? Where, in the time of pain and trial, do we discover God's love enfolding us? Where do we drink in the "perfume of chastity" and learn to love with a free heart? Where do we grow in hunger to give our life for God and for the world's salvation? Only in the gentle arms of our mother prayer who alone "fills the vessel of our heart with the blood of the Lamb and crowns it with fire," the fire of God's own love.[127] This mother who did not forsake Catherine even in death became the mother she gave to her friends as her last heritage: "Be men and women of persevering prayer."[128]

[126]R 3.4, p. 335.

[127]Let T 353 to Monna Catella, Cecia, and Caterina Dentice.

[128]R 3.4, p. 335.

6

The Blood of Jesus:
Mercy for the Human Heart

"Surely goodness and mercy shall follow me all the days of my life" (Ps 23:6). Catherine's prayer uncovered for her the depth of our human desire to live bathed in mercy. In the secret places within us where we bear wounds that cry out for healing, the very word "mercy" has power to draw tears to our eyes. We long for a mercy that will wash us in rivers of forgiveness and healing; but, even in our hope for it, we know how deeply and radically mercy is granted only as sheer, undeserved gift.

Our bodies cry out for a mercy that is tangible, and yet our spirits thirst for a mercy deeper than created reality can impart; we need a mercy that we touch and taste not only with our bodies but also with our inmost spirits. Yet does the human heart know this kind of mercy? For Catherine, the words of Psalm 23, far from alluding to a human longing lovely in its aspiration yet unattainable in its fulfillment, proclaim rather the reality in which "we live and move and have our being" (Act 17:28). With the apostles and every disciple after them Catherine found in Jesus' blood the love of God made human, the mercy of God made visible.

For if we long for mercy, we have only to bathe our entire being in the blood of Jesus, the cleansing, healing liquid which alone "shatters the diamond" of our resistance and softens our heart to God and one another.[1] No matter how grievous, our every sin can be washed clean by this saving blood that bathes us in the "expansiveness of God's charity and forgiveness." The Father tells Catherine that he forbids us to think of our sins "either in general or specifically without calling to mind the blood and the greatness of my mercy."[2] Even if we have spent our entire life in sin, we must cry out with Magdalen for the mercy infinitely more powerful than our sin: "I will hide myself in his blood, and so my wickedness will be consumed."[3] Catherine thus asks the Father to wash our soul's face with his only Son's blood that, in place of discouragement and despair, we may offer him "bright face and undivided soul."[4]

Catherine's Mystical Grace: Thirst for the Blood of Jesus

It was through key mystical experiences in her own life that Catherine's thirst grew for the outpouring of Jesus' blood upon the world. We have seen how the bitterness which repulsed her turned to unspeakable sweetness when she forced herself to drink the putrid water in which she had washed the ulcerous sores of an abusive woman. In return for the love she had shown her sister the Lord invited her to drink mystically from his side, in this way satisfying her deepest thirst for infinite good.[5] Raymond later understood Catherine's experience as a revelation of the Lord's desire for union with each one of us: "When they drink of you," he

[1] D 4, p. 32.
[2] D 55, p. 124.
[3] D 66, p. 125.
[4] Pr 8, p. 65.
[5] R 3.6, p. 376.

cries out in praise to the Lord, "they take you to themselves more quickly and more eagerly, and you become one with them more readily and perfectly."[6]

Catherine also began to realize that the blood poured out from Jesus' body has bathed us all in the fire of the Spirit's love.[7] The inseparability of water and fire in the universe itself became a mirror for her of Jesus' blood commingled with the fire of the spirit whose love urged him to die for us: "The fire hidden under our ashes began to show itself completely and generously by splitting open his most holy body on the wood of the cross."[8]

We have seen how the force of this fire broke through even into Catherine's body. In 1370, her heart seemed to enter into the Lord's side and become so united with his that she could only cry out, "Lord you have wounded my heart."[9] Again, while in Pisa, she felt his wounds piercing her hands, feet, and heart with light—a grace whose pain she experienced continually in her body.[10]

And because Jesus had poured out his blood for her, Catherine longed to give her own life for him in an act of unreserved love. "They have triumphed...by the blood of the Lamb and by the witness of their martyrdom" (Rev 12:11). The early Christian martyrs stood before her mind's eye,[11] inviting her to join their company in the blood of Jesus which alone gives peace to those at war.[12] "And you, Jesus Christ, our reconciler, our refashioner, our redeemer—You turned our great war with God into a great peace."[13]

As she witnessed the increasing civil and ecclesiastical division around her, Catherine grew convinced that the blood of

[6]R 2.4, p. 156.

[7]Let T 270 to Pope Gregory XI.

[8]Pr 19, p. 172.

[9]R 2.6, p. 180.

[10]R 2.6, p. 186.

[11]Let T 319 to Stefano di Corrado Maconi.

[12]Let T 295 to Raymond of Capua.

[13]Pr 1, p. 17.

Jesus himself, crying out in the blood of even one martyr, would pour out the divine mercy upon the world. One remedy alone could shatter our hearts of stone: "I see no way in which they can break except through the blood."[14] The blood of Jesus shed in a torrent of love increasingly fed Catherine's desire to wash clean the Church's marred face with her own blood. Yet she was not to know that gift. We recall how, in 1378, the martyrdom that lay within her grasp eluded her. The man intent on her death found himself paralyzed before her radiant courage and could not raise the sword against her. But instead of rejoicing, Catherine could only weep, for the "multitude" of her sins, as she wrote later to Raymond, had rendered her unworthy of a martyr's death.[15]

Three years earlier, Catherine had witnessed what a death in and for the Lord could mean. In 1375, the same year in which she had received mystically the Lord's wounds, a Sienese youth, Niccolò di Tuldo, had been condemned to beheading for a political offense. Hearing of his bitterness and despair, Catherine went to strengthen and comfort the imprisoned young man; on the morning of the execution she accompanied him to Mass and assisted at his first Communion in a long time. The grace of this Eucharist so filled Niccolò with God's mercy that his rage turned inexplicably to contentment, and he began to long for the death that would unite him to his Lord.

The youth begged Catherine to stay at his side during the execution. "So it shall not be otherwise than well with me. And I die content."[16] As Catherine ministered to him, she sensed how fragrant an offering in the Church his death would be if he went to it bathed in forgiveness and peace. She encouraged him to go to his execution as to his wedding feast, covered with Jesus' blood. Catherine's words pierced the young man's heart. Fear and sadness gave way to an

[14]Let T 296 to Don Giovanni of the Cells; Scudder, p. 267.

[15]Let T 295 to Raymond of Capua; Scudder, p. 258.

[16]Let T 273 (DT 31) to Raymond of Capua; Scudder, p. 112.

interior joy so deep that he called the place of justice a "holy place" and begged Catherine to await him there. As she did, her own desire to die for the Lord so deepened that she longed to take Niccolò's place. When he arrived, she gently blessed him, speaking to him of Jesus' blood; within moments, she received his severed head into her hands.

Immediately afterwards, Catherine wrote to Raymond recounting this experience. At Niccolò's death, she seemed to see Jesus bathed in his own blood and the fire of infinite love. In turn, he drew to himself the young man's blood filled with his desire for Jesus. Fire met fire. As mercy alone had converted Niccolò, Jesus now led him to his open side, full of mercy. Catherine felt the sweetness of the Lord's desire to receive the youth into his heart; bathed in his own blood made powerful by Jesus' blood, Niccolò approached Jesus' open side.

The youth then seemed to turn his face toward Catherine and to give a parting sign "sweet enough to draw a thousand hearts." Having tasted the sweetness of God, Niccolò did as the bride who, at the threshold of the spouse's home, turns her gaze toward the companions who have assisted her, and gives a gentle sign of love and gratitude. "And the hands of the Holy Spirit locked him within" the paradise of the Lord's heart. This vision filled Catherine with such peace that she could not bear to remove the youth's blood from her clothes, so fragrant an offering it seemed to her. "Ah me,... I will say no more," she writes. "I stayed on the earth with the greatest envy."[17]

In the bitterness of Niccolò's death, Catherine experienced the power of Jesus' blood to transform both his own sin and that of his enemies. "Ask, and it will be given you" (Lk 11:9); convinced that God remains true to his promise, she began to make her life a living intercession for a new outpouring of Jesus' blood upon the world. She realized that this blood is ours, that God has made it a bath for us and will not refuse it to anyone who asks. "Put into the scales the price of your

[17]*Ibid.*; Scudder, p. 114.

Son's blood," she begs the Father; "it is this blood that your servants, hungry as they are, are asking for at this door. They are asking you through this blood to be merciful to the world."[18]

Catherine began to steep herself in the mystery of God's mercy which longs to reach down to our lowliness and to help us in our need. "Oh very sweet love. How mercy is proper to you!" When the human race first sinned, God did not command the earth to swallow us up nor the beasts to devour us, but instead clothed us in mercy, indeed, lavished on us a mercy infinitely greater than the effects of our sin.[19] The Father forbids us to expect less of him today: "Keep expanding your heart and your affection in the immeasurable greatness of my mercy."[20] And Catherine in turn urges us: "Hide yourself under the wings of the mercy of God, for it is more inclined to pardon than you are to sin. Bathe yourself in the blood of Christ."[21]

In a particularly tender letter written at the behest of the woman's brother, Catherine urges a prostitute to run to Mary, "the mother of compassion and mercy." Mary leads us to Jesus, and Jesus begs us to take shelter in his wounds, where we find only the fire of charity and the bath of his blood. "Our sweet Savior will not despise you." Catherine asks the woman to think of the "sweet and tender" Magdalen who boldly trusted that Jesus' mercy far exceeded her sin. Thinking not of her shame but only of how she could find his mercy, she threw herself at his feet. Her humility and trust won for her this "sweet word" from the Lord: "Go in peace and do not sin any more" (Lk 7:50; Jn 8:11). "Do the same, my very sweet daughter," Catherine writes. "Give to him your heart, your soul, your body." Catherine tenderly assures the woman that her brother will provide for her and

---

[18]D 134, p. 276.

[19]Let T 173 to a religious who left his order.

[20]D 66, p. 124.

[21]Let T 173 to a religious who left his order.

that the Lord himself will care for all her needs.[22]

As she counseled others, Catherine saw how we hold back from Magdalen's boldness in trusting God's mercy. Fearing death, we think, "My life merits nothing but hell; I have done very little good and much sin." Despair tempts us to see only our guilt rather than God's mercy. Yet we must cry out with Magdalen, "I hope in God; he will pardon my sins and give me his grace." Now is the time to begin anew. If death comes before we seem ready, we must boldly entrust ourselves to Jesus, since there exists "no comparison between God's mercy" and our sin. The iniquity of the entire world disappears as a "drop of vinegar" when cast into the ocean of God's love. If we would but repent, the guilt of the whole universe would be devoured by the sea of God's love and as a mere drop would disappear in its embrace.[23]

Dying into the Mercy of God

Catherine began to understand that hope in God's mercy during our lifetime draws us all the more to make our death a radical act of trust. As we approach death, we come face to face with our need and sin. "Yet," the Father tells Catherine, "their only hope is to put their trust in my mercy if only this one time in their whole life." If we humbly confess our sin, "what remains is mercy." We are called to make of our lives a radical act of trust so that at the point of death we will plunge ourselves not into the pit of despair but into the abyss of God's mercy.

Of every sin, despair alone finally closes us off from God for it "spurns" the Lord by considering our sin greater than his mercy. This is why the Father assures Catherine, "It is my will that they should put their trust in my mercy even at the point of death, after they have spent their life in wickedness." Despair alone leads us to the mouth of hell. When we

[22]Let T 276 to a prostitute in Perugia.
[23]Let T 314 to Monna Costanza Soderini.

repent and trust in God's mercy, however, we find only mercy: "My mercy is incomparably greater than all the sins anyone could commit."[24]

Death refuses us "refuge" in our own virtue because we "have none." "Your only refuge will be my mercy. . . . trust in the blood and in my mercy." This radical trust draws us not to presumption but to conversion and trust in God's power to heal and change us. If at the moment of death guilt assails us, if we feel only fear and discouragement at the emptiness of our hands and lives before God, we are still to surrender ourselves to God in a supreme act of trust. "No one ought to despair. No, reach out trustingly for the blood, no matter what sins you have committed, for my mercy, which you receive in the blood, is incomparably greater than all the sins that have ever been committed in the world."[25]

The God who lavishes his mercy upon the world even in the face of its worst sin deserves the supreme honor of our own lavish trust in that mercy.[26] For the despair which rejects God's mercy far exceeds the guilt of any other sin we could commit: "The despair of Judas displeased me more and was a greater insult to my Son than his betrayal had been."[27] Thus, the Lord so yearns for our trust at the point of death that he employs the "gentle trick" of nurturing constant trust in us now; living in hope now, we will not easily let go of it when inner voices of reproach confront us at death.[28]

With this confidence, we will approach death itself with joy and peace.[29] Bathed in the blood of Jesus, we will pass gently through death's door and find ourselves in the heart of God, the sea of peace.[30] We will not turn back to look at

---

[24]D 132, p. 268.
[25]D 129, p. 260.
[26]D 132, p. 268.
[27]D 37, p. 79.
[28]D 132, p. 268.
[29]Let T 314 to Monna Costanza Soderini.
[30]D 82, p. 152.

our own past virtues, but gaze instead at the blood where we find God's mercy. And as we filled our memory with Jesus' blood during our life, so in death we will immerse ourselves in this same blood. We will lift out the arms of our hope and grasp with the hands of our love the very heart of God, and in this way enter into heaven even before we die. Having lived in trust and love, we will experience the joy of finding ourselves "so gently brought to this passing,"[31] for we will awaken to Jesus gazing at us not with reproach but only with the most tender compassion and mercy.[32]

In heaven we will discover, too, the scars of Jesus crying out as a living plea to the Father for mercy upon the world. The wounds Jesus suffered at our hands on earth now radiate as imprints of love for us in heaven. In the same way, our own sufferings endured on earth will shine as "adornments" on our risen body. Our soul's fullness will shine outwardly, imprinting on our body the joyous fruit of our trials; like reflections in a mirror, the very pain and heartache we experienced will manifest gloriously the Lord's own death and resurrection in our body.[33]

The Heart of Jesus: Love Made Visible

"When I am lifted up from the earth, I will draw all. . .to myself" (Jn 12:32). Nothing in the universe draws us more irresistibly than love. In the cross of Jesus Catherine discovered not the repugnant horror of death pushing us away, but the gracious face of love drawing us close. No human power nailed Jesus to the cross, for earthly forces could not bind him to the wood had his own love not held him fast.[34] A tortured death thus paradoxically shines as the revelation of the most profound beauty: "He bows his head to greet you,

---

[31]D 131, p. 264.

[32]D 41, p. 85.

[33]D 42, p. 86.

[34]Let T 253 to Trincio De' Trinci da Fuligno and Corrado his brother.

wears the crown of thorns to adorn you, stretches out his arms to embrace you, lets his feet be nailed that he may stand with you."[35] Raised on high before the gaze of the entire universe, the cross of Jesus unveils infinite love vulnerable to the last measure of self-giving, as love alone shines forth from every part of Jesus' torn body.

Yet the source of love, Jesus' heart, no one could see. "They pierced his side with a lance and immediately there came forth blood and water" (Jn 18:34). In prayer, Catherine began to understand the inevitably finite nature of Jesus' suffering; his death ended his pain. But no amount of love could manifest the infinite love of God's own heart. For this reason alone, Jesus suffered the soldiers to pierce his side after his death. "I wanted you to see my inmost heart, so that you would see that I loved you more than finite suffering could show."[36] In the opening of his side, Jesus unveils to us his heart, source of unbounded love: "There you find my heart's secret and it shows you...how I love you."[37] Our own blood contains our finite life force, but the blood of Jesus' slain body flows as the human sacrament pouring out God's infinite love upon the world. More than any finite suffering could show, the blood of Jesus unveils to our eyes the length to which God's love will go for us.

If Jesus had died even a thousand deaths for us, we would still fail to grasp the infinite depths of God's love for us. But when the side of God's own Son was torn open to pour forth the last measure of his blood, we could know finally and without doubt the truth of God's mercy toward us. The blood of Jesus has rendered infinite mercy visible. Flowing from every part of his wounded body, his blood opens to our eyes our own capacity to destroy, and the infinitely greater capacity of God to heal.[38] And since we sin with every part of our body, his blood has flowed from every part

[35]D 128, p. 252.

[36]D 75, p. 138.

[37]*Ibid.*, p. 139.

[38]Let T 315 to Don Pietro da Milano, Carthusian.

of his body, redeeming us not simply "with just a single drop of his blood . . . but with this whole body's pain and blood."[39] Bathed on the cross with his own blood, Jesus now makes of his blood a bath of love to wash and to heal the very ones whose sin has killed him:[40] "I have made the blood . . . to be a bath to wash away your sins."[41]

Catherine began to understand that we ourselves form the living vessel to receive the blood Jesus pours out upon the world,[42] blood which not only reveals how infinitely loved we are but which also fills us with the very power of that love. For the boundless capacity of God to transform us meets our own unlimited capacity to be made new by the fire flowing from Jesus' open side.[43] The Father thus urges us to cling to Jesus the way a child clings to its mother's breast, finding in his blood the love and intimacy we need.[44] Jesus himself will wash us in his blood, bathe us in forgiveness, and hide us in the cavern of his open side.[45]

In the wounded side of Jesus, Catherine found the place which enfolds the entire world in mercy. "Stretched out on the cross you have embraced us. For us you have made a cavern in your open side, where we might have a refuge."[46] Reposing here, we discover the peace of the home we need never leave. Mary Magdalen knew the depths of this grace, for she made the heart of Jesus her only treasure and dwelling place. By filling her mind and heart with him, Magdalen covered herself with Jesus' blood; she washed herself clean

[39]Pr 9, p. 73.

[40]Let T 262 to Monna Tora Gambacorta of Pisa.

[41]D 126, p. 246.

[42]Let T 102 to Raymond of Capua.

[43]Let T 112 to Monna Benedetta Salimbeni of Rome, who had suffered through both the death of her first husband a short time after her wedding, and the death of the man to whom she afterwards became engaged.

[44]Let T 86 to the Abbess of the Monastery of Santa Maria delli Scalzi at Florence.

[45]Let T 163 to Monna Franceschina.

[46]Pr 19, p. 176.

with it and bathed her inmost being in the perfume of his mercy.[47]

A Continuing Baptism of Blood

The forgiveness Jesus gave to Magdalen he now showers on us through the sacraments. Catherine pictures the Church as the abundantly rich "wine cellar" containing the precious drink of Christ's blood from which all the sacraments gain their life-giving power.[48] Knowing "how people sin because of their weakness," the heart of God has given us confession precisely as an "ongoing baptism of blood."[49] For even when the gravity of our sin tempts us to despair, confession washes us clean in the blood that outweighs every sin that has been committed or ever could be.[50] So powerfully does this sacrament bathe us in the flood of God's mercy that it can make of us a new creation.[51]

Catherine realizes that the shame we feel in our sin makes us reluctant to bare our weakness before another's eyes. We keep away from the cleansing waters of this sacrament of mercy because we fear that in exposing our sin, we expose ourselves as worthless. But Catherine asks her disciples to gaze at the "humility of God" revealed in Jesus. On the cross the body of Jesus lies utterly exposed before eyes of mockery and derision. The vulnerability of a God driven by love to such defenselessness becomes a river of mercy to soften our own resistance.[52]

God's mercy is thus filled with paradox: what causes us shame evokes only love from God, and the sin that we think

[47]Let T 163 to Monna Franceschina.

[48]D 115, p. 215.

[49]D 75, p. 138.

[50]Let 343 to Rainaldo da Capua, perhaps the father of Raymond of Capua, and noted for his pursuit of sacred studies.

[51]D 75, p. 139.

[52]Let T 234 (DT 82) to Buonaccurso di Lapo.

drives God from us instead draws him close to us. In the
pain we encounter as we grow toward our identity in God,
we can find strength and comfort in Jesus' own experience:
"O gentle loving Word,...you yourself had to suffer in
order to enter into your very self." [53] The God who formed
every part of our being intimately knows and cherishes us;
our very weakness invites the flood of his mercy upon us. If
we are estranged from God and the Church, this sacrament
reunites us in mercy and peace, for the blood of Jesus lavished upon us in confession makes the sick well and raises
the dead to new life.[54]

"Come to Me and Drink" (Jn 7:37)

As she found in the sacrament of reconciliation a continu-
ing baptism of blood, Catherine discovered in the Eucharist
the power of Jesus' blood to fill us with the very life of God.
Raymond admits that Catherine regarded him with such
gratitude precisely because he never denied her the Eucharist. Realizing the intensity of her hunger for the Lord's body
and blood, he obtained Gregory XI's permission for a priest
to travel with Catherine to hear her confession, to celebrate
the Eucharist, and to give her Communion daily.[55] Because
of her own experience of intimacy with the Lord in Communion, she urges her disciples to let nothing keep them
from this "sweet sacrament." To her good friend Ristoro
Canigiani she writes that no feeling of unworthiness should
keep us from the Lord's body and blood. Even if we have
performed the greatest deeds of virtue in the world, in the
end we shall still be unworthy. If we wait for the time when
we will be worthy to feed on God we shall wait throughout
our life in vain. We are unworthy of God. But God is worthy

[53]Pr 20, p. 190.

[54]D 108, p. 202.

[55]R 2.2, p. 291.

of us and desires to give himself to us as food; with his own worth Jesus makes worthy those who desire him.[56]

"Do this in remembrance of me, ... This cup which is poured out for you is the new covenant in my blood" (Lk 22:19, 20). Jesus bestows on his community nothing less than his own life as the new covenant binding us irrevocably to God. The blood of an animal sprinkled on the altar and on the people had sealed the covenant of love and fidelity between God and the Hebrew community (Ex 24:3-9). The victim eaten by the people symbolized the one life they shared with God. Yet this participation in the covenant meal excluded a sharing in the blood of the victim. Blood contains the life principle and thus belongs only to God, author of life (Lev 1:5). The blood of the victim sprinkled as purification on the people remained unconsumed.

Broken again and again by human infidelity, the covenant before Jesus was renewed with the blood of animals symbolizing union but powerless to render the people faithful to that union (Heb 9:12-22). The Scriptures unfold the painful story of countless animals offered in sacrifice with blood that could not change human hearts. Against this tragic backdrop, New Testament authors behold in Jesus crucified the Lamb whose outpoured blood has reversed the course of history. The blood of this Lamb conveys infinite power to seal forever the union of God with his people. In Jesus, the human partner to the covenant becomes finally and irrevocably faithful.

The Hebrews were forbidden to consume the blood of the animals they sacrificed; the blood, seat of life, belongs to God alone. In a paradox of divine mercy, Jesus not only permits but commands his community to drink his blood. "If you do not eat the flesh of the Son of Man and drink his blood, you will not have life in you" (Jn 6:25). The life principle surges in the blood; those who drink of Jesus' blood drink the power of his life as their own. In Jesus the life of God and his people commingle and become one:

[56]Let T 258 to Ristoro Canigiani.

whoever "eats my flesh and drinks my blood lives in me and I in him" (Jn 6:57).

In company with the early Christian community, Catherine began to experience increasingly the power of Jesus' blood to assuage our deepest hunger and thirst.[57] As she watched others appear to possess the entire world and still live unsatisfied, she grew to understand that the inner ache and restlessness we experience are the fruit of the Holy Spirit's cry within us. We are made for unbounded love; and in the blood of Jesus alone do we find the infinite love and mercy able to satisfy our every human longing.[58]

"I created your soul with a capacity for loving—so much so that you cannot live without love. Indeed, love is your food."[59] Catherine began to understand that the Eucharist feeds us with nothing less than the fire of God's love. But we who receive Communion are to meet fire with fire. As we bring the flame of our own desire and love to this sacrament, we will leave with as much as we desire, for each of us partakes of the same infinite charity that in no way diminishes the more it is shared. The one fire of love inflaming the blood of Christ becomes a fire burning in each of us individually and in all of us together, until the entire world grows to share in its light and warmth.[60]

Having experienced the power of Jesus' blood in her own life, Catherine began increasingly to beg for the mercy of this blood upon those who resist God. "Unlock and shatter the hardened hearts of your creatures," she cries out to the Father. "I beg you to force their wills and dispose them to want what they do not want. I ask this of your infinite mercy."[61] Catherine herself had experienced how deeply the bath of this blood heals our selfishness and bathes our

---

[57] *Ibid.*

[58] Let T 87 to Monna Giovanna Pazzi, from one of the most noble families of Florence, and a frequent companion of Catherine's.

[59] D 110, p. 208.

[60] *Ibid.*, pp. 208-09.

[61] D 134, pp. 275-76.

inmost beings. Nourishing ourselves with the blood of Jesus, we feed on mercy itself. If we have been unfaithful, the blood baptizes us again; if we have grown indifferent, the memory of Jesus' blood reawakens lost gratitude; and when our zeal has grown cold, the blood warms and inflames us anew.

In the blood of Jesus Catherine discovered an infinite treasury of joy for our hearts, for even in the pain of a broken or estranged relationship, the blood of Jesus floods us with a love intimate enough to bathe us in healing. "I deceived myself when I sought to find happiness only in creatures," she writes to Raymond; "I will drink of their love in the blood and so taste peace in war, and sweetness in bitterness."[62] Those who have experienced the gift of human tenderness, as well as those who have been deprived of it, can find in the heart of Jesus the closeness and joy which God alone can give: "Not as the world gives do I give to you... Your hearts will rejoice, and no one will take your joy from you" (Jn 14:27; 16:22).

Catherine had inspired Niccolò to approach his death as his wedding feast. She began to view the meaning of the life and death of each of us in the same way, as the wedding feast of God with us. Jesus has wedded each of us with a nuptial band unlike any ring of silver or gold, for the wedding band of his own flesh irrevocably binds us to God, and his own blood pledges his fidelity to us.[63] Because each one of us is the chosen bride redeemed by the blood of God's Son, Jesus calls us to live in the joy and thanksgiving of the bride, washing ourselves clean with his blood, breaking the hard-

[62] Let T 102 to Raymond of Capua.

[63] Let T 143 (DT 39) to Queen Giovanna of Naples. In what seems to be a comparison original with her, Catherine here pictures the "espousal" of Jesus with the human race at his circumcision: "Oh Jesus, gentlest love, as a sign that you had espoused us you gave us the ring of your most holy and tender flesh at the time of your holy circumcision on the eighth day...on the eighth day enough flesh was taken from him to make a circlet of a ring; to give us a sure hope of payment in full he began by paying this pledge. And we received the full payment on the wood of the most holy cross" (Noffke, trans.). On the feast of the Circumcision, 1380, Catherine prayed: "Today again in your mercy you espouse our souls to you with the ring of your flesh, the ring of your charity" (Pr 25, p. 215).

ness of our heart with it, and filling our entire being with its gladness.[64]

"You who have been far apart have been brought close by the blood of Christ" (Eph 2:13). Catherine's mystical experience of the power of Jesus' blood, her pleas to drink and to bathe in it, express the truth which had possessed the first Christians. The blood of a crucified Lord opens our gaze to a love whose unspeakable force could be shown in no other way (1 Cor 1:22). Pierced and crushed for sins not his own, the slain Lamb bears and heals the wounds of the entire world and in his own blood reconciles and weds us to God (Is 53:3-7): "This bridegroom, the spotless Lamb, poured out his blood freely from every member and with it washed away...the sin of humankind his spouse."[65] Precisely because Catherine found in this blood both the healing and the tenderness for which the human heart is made, she offers to each one of us the invitation she extended to Raymond after Niccolò's death: "I impose upon you nothing save to see yourselves drowned in the blood and flame poured from the side of the Son of God."[66]

---

[64]Let T 193 to Lorenzo del Pino of Bologna.

[65]Let T 143 (DT 39) to Queen Giovanna of Naples; Noffke, trans.

[66]Let T 273 (DT 31) to Raymond of Capua; Scudder, p. 114.

7

The Two Wings of Love

"Beloved, if God so loved us, we also ought to love one another." No one "has ever seen God; if we love one another, God abides in us and his love is perfected in us" (1 Jn 4:11, 12). In company with all who have desired closeness with the living God, Catherine had to learn the inseparable relationship between intimacy with God and with others. For the mercy God has lavished on us we are commanded to spend just as generously on our brothers and sisters: "This is my commandment, that you love one another as I have loved you" (Jn 15:12).

In loving the truth made flesh, Catherine could not escape the call to union with the living flesh he has become. Her vocation thus unfolds as the story of a woman who learned with her life that, far from hindering our intimacy with God, unselfish love and communion with others truly unite us with the God who not only lives among us but who has also become literally one of us (Jn 1:14).

The Call to Love

Many of Catherine's contemporaries were deeply scandal-
ized by the great number of men and women who left everything to be always in her company. They were married and
unmarried; religious, priests, and hermits; aristocrats and
common folk; illiterate and scholars. And they gladly
accepted the name which skeptics applied to them: *cateri-
nati*, "be-Catherined." Indeed, Catherine's capacity for
attracting people to her amazed even her critics. The depth
of her affection spontaneously showed itself in her tenderness toward her nieces and nephews, whom she once said she
could never tire of holding and caressing. Her ardor and
warmth embraced all who came to her, and in every city
there were those who welcomed her as a dear friend. And
because none of her *famiglia* seemed willing to be deprived
of her presence any more than they had to, there were often
scores of people who accompanied Catherine in her travels,
and many more who wanted to.

Yet Catherine's extraordinary capacity for love was not
attained without cost. Because her heart needed expansion
and purification if there was to be room in it for others, she,
too, knew the human struggle of learning how to love. The
Catherine who addressed a friend as "my sweetest, dearest,
my best beloved brother, whom I love as my own soul,"
earlier in her life had to be forced even to speak to people;
and the Catherine accused by her critics of excessive fond-
ness for others' company had once desired to live only as a
hermit.

We have seen, however, how formative experiences in her
young adulthood pushed Catherine to relationship with others. Inwardly prompted to leave her solitude when she was
about twenty, Catherine let go of her extreme reluctance
only at the Lord's promise that he would bind her even more
closely to himself through communion with others. Just as a
person cannot walk with one foot or a bird fly with one
wing, he told her, she would fail to love at all if she tried to
love the unseen God but not the brothers and sisters whom

she could see. For about the next three years, Catherine devoted herself to charitable works in and near her home, attending to the needs of the poor and sick; yet contact with others still cost her deeply, and as soon as she could she would return to her room to be alone with the Lord.

Other formative experiences, however, changed not only Catherine's actions but also her heart. We recall how, in July of 1370, at the age of twenty-three, she experienced in response to her prayer for a pure heart the Lord's giving her his own. With his heart she would conceive an unheard-of love for others, scandalizing many with the boldness of her love and the paradox of her life. Yet the Lord willed to delay her coming to him so that many could be converted through her. As she later told Raymond, her profound love for others should offend no one, since she had bought them at the highest of all prices: "For their sake I have been separated from the Lord."

Again, we have seen how, in 1375, after experiencing a kind of death in which she received the Lord's own wounds, Catherine confided to Raymond that she was "no longer the same person." An inner fire seemed to burn within her, "renewing and rejuvenating" her inmost being; such a "boundless" love for others filled her that she would "undergo death itself with joy and gladness" for their salvation.[1]

"Love One Another" (1 Jn 4:11)

Catherine began to see how love itself begets love. Finding herself loved so generously by God, she wanted not only to love God in return, but also to love him with his own self-lessness.[2] Yet this is precisely what she could not do, since our love for God can be only a grateful response to love first received. "I love you without being loved and without any

[1] R 2.6, p. 176.
[2] R 2.1, p. 116.

self-interest. . . . Because I loved you without being loved by you, even before you existed,. . .you cannot repay me."[3] As Catherine learned, however, we do have a way of loving God with the same unconditional love lavished upon us. "Beloved, if God so loved us, we also ought to love one another" (1 Jn 4:11). Finally, we can return selfless love to God by reaching out to others, "loving them without being loved by them," and loving them precisely because God loves them.[4]

"Where two or three are gathered in my name, I am in the midst of them" (Mt 18:20). Catherine's own experience showed her that God is not "in the midst" of someone cut off from others through selfish isolation; "one alone" is thus excluded from the Lord's companionship: "Those who are wrapped up in selfish love of themselves are alone, mere nothings, because they are cut off from my grace and from charity for their neighbor."[5]

Catherine grew to understand that the God who easily could have made each of us self-sufficient has chosen to create us in the image of the unspeakably rich triune communion. We are made to need one another, and without the love and gifts of our brothers and sisters, we literally cannot live. "I wanted to make you dependent on one another so that each of you would be my minister, dispensing the graces and gifts you have received from me."[6]

Our attempts to live isolated from others end by destroying our own identity, for we have been created to live in the very charity that inflames the heart of God: "The conformity between person and person is such that when they do not love each other they cut themselves off from their own nature."[7] But even more, the Lord has so identified himself with us that our love for one another truly binds us to him as well:[8] "I have put you among your neighbors so that you can

[3]D 89, p. 165.

[4]*Ibid.*

[5]D 54, p. 107.

[6]D 7, p. 38.

[7]Pr 22, p. 198.

[8]Let T 53 to Monna Agnesa Malavolti.

do for them what you cannot do for me;...love them without any concern for thanks and without looking for any profit for yourself. And whatever you do for them I will consider done for me."[9]

Special Faith and Love

Perhaps her friendship with Raymond of Capua formed the school in which Catherine grew most in her ability to love. Seventeen years older than Catherine, former chaplain for the nuns at Montepulciano and destined to head the Dominican Order after her death, Raymond was assigned as lecturer in theology at the Dominican house in Siena in 1374. For the next three years he was Catherine's confessor and closest confidante.

In 1377, however, he was appointed prior of the Church of the Minerva in Rome. His departure was heart-breaking for Catherine, and her letters during this time show how much his absence cost her. But in 1379, with her death less than a year away, Catherine herself was finally summoned to Rome by Gregory's successor, Pope Urban VI. Yet her joy at being reunited with Raymond soon felt again the sting of separation. In an attempt to win France's allegiance away from the anti-pope Clement VII, Urban sent Raymond on a mission to the French king.

Their last visit before his departure was to hold immense significance for Raymond and Catherine. After speaking together for many hours, Catherine gently sent him away with the words, "Go now with God, for I feel that never again in this life will we have a long talk together like this." Sensing the sorrow the future held for them, Catherine later came to the place of departure for a final good-bye and let her tears and blessing speak what her voice could not. As the ship set sail, "she knelt and prayed, and then she made the Sign of the Cross with her hand, weeping as she did so."

[9]D 64, p. 121.

Only after Catherine's death did Raymond understand the unspoken significance of these tears, for it was as if she were saying, "Go in confidence but know that we will never see one another again in this life." And, Raymond recalls, it was as Catherine had intimated: "I went away; she remained behind, and before I came back she had gone to heaven."[10]

Although Catherine's heart was heavy at seeing Raymond leave, she cherished other hopes for him: that he would succeed in winning France's allegiance to Urban, and, if not, that he would die a martyr on that mission. Raymond himself, however, somehow eluded Catherine's passion for martyrdom, and frightened by the prospect of the French troops awaiting him, he turned back at the border. If Catherine's heart was wounded by his departure, it was broken by this failure in courage on the part of her beloved friend. Aware of how deeply his cowardice must have disappointed her, he wrote to Catherine of his fear that she would love him less because of it.

Catherine's response could not hold back the depth of her own love and commitment to him. We love others with a "general" love and faith, she writes; but God sometimes gives also a "special" faith and love "to those who love one another more intimately: like this, which beyond the common love has established between us two a close particular love."[11] God grants a mutual love and trust in one another so that each friend may find support in the burdens she or he must bear for the Church. The friends whom God joins in this kind of relationship are not to doubt the other's love nor to lessen their own love for any reason but rather are to support and love one another faithfully. And if separation or their friend's imperfections weaken their love, it is a sign that both God and the friend are loved with only an imperfect love.[12]

[10]R 3.1, pp. 313-14.
[11]Let T 344 to Raymond of Capua; Scudder, p. 326.
[12]Cf. D 144, pp. 302-03.

Catherine goes on to say that she understands the fear and inadequacy Raymond must have felt before the task assigned him. But his fear that his weakness would cause her to love him less showed that he doubted her love. In fact, however, it was he whose love grew less by his doubting her, and her love which grew stronger. "You did not see aright,...it was you who showed that I had grown to love more, and you less. For the love with which I love myself, with that I love you....I show a love increased in me towards you, and not waning."[13] With all of her heart she wishes he had been faithful, and she prays that only she will know of his cowardice; but she will stay faithful to him, laboring for his good and doing all in her power to help him attain holiness—and martyrdom if possible. Catherine closes by asking his patience with her faults and assuring him that only love had ever motivated her words to him.

"I have called you friends, for all that I have heard from my Father I have made known to you" (Jn 15:15). Could others who knew of the closeness between Catherine and Raymond have suspected the painful matters which both had to work out together after his failure at Genoa? Yet Catherine had found in Jn 14-17 the paradigm for friendships given by God: friends lay down their lives for one another, admitting the loved one into the secrets of their heart and saying with their lives, "All that is mine is yours" (Jn 17:10).

"This is how it is with very dear friends. Their loving affection makes them two bodies with one soul, because love transforms one into what one loves. And if these souls are made one soul [with me], nothing can be kept hidden from them."[14] With these words the Father unveiled to Catherine the mystery of God's friendship with us. And when the same words describe in an analogous way the human friendships given by God, they speak of a communion that participates in God's own inner life. But as Catherine herself discovered,

---

[13]Let T 344 to Raymond of Capua; Scudder, p. 327.
[14]D 60, pp. 115-16.

no one gains a gift this invaluable without cost. "You will know the truth and the truth will make you free" (Jn 8:31). This kind of communion requires not only continual growth in our own identity before God, but also the vulnerability of a mutual trust and openness which bring our weaknesses as well as strengths into the light before one another.

Unselfish Love

As she prayed for the people whose pain and suffering she bore in her own heart, Catherine saw that we who have been created by love itself cannot live without love. Because we are made for love, we hunger for it more deeply than for food; the nameless human ache that wells up from within us cries out for nothing less than love.[15] Catherine realized, however, that only "perfect love" can satisfy us. We are made for and need a love that values us not as an extension of another, but precisely as ourselves. Free of manipulative and possessive needs, this kind of unselfish love does not absorb us into another's identity and plans, but rather calls us forth to grow in our own personal uniqueness.

Catherine realized, too, that our human wholeness requires not simply being loved but also actively loving in this way. "But you will say to me, 'Since I have no such love, and without it I am powerless, how can I get it?' I will tell you. Love is had only by loving. If you want love, you must begin by loving—I mean you must want to love."[16] Since we are made of love, we do, in fact, "always want to love."[17] Yet of ourselves, we have the capacity only for what Catherine calls "imperfect love," a love that reaches out to others only to meet our own need rather than to give to others from our inner abundance and security.

[15]D 51, p. 103.

[16]Let T 29 (DT 18) to Regina della Scala, wife of Bernabo Visconti, lord of Milan; Noffke, trans.

[17]D 51, p. 103.

Our naturally self-centered love for God and for others looks out for its own advantage and withdraws at the least sign of difficulty or inconvenience.[18] Rather than opening us to true communion with others, this "imperfect love" centers us on the narrow world of our own self, for it reaches out to others only when it suits our own advantage.[19] When we see others' infidelities or faults, we resort to a "proud humility," withdrawing our love with the excuse, "I will not pay these people any more attention, or trouble myself any more about them. I will keep entirely to myself; I do not wish to hurt either myself or them."[20]

The signs of a self-centered love thus manifest themselves: "If you are distressed when it seems to you that you are being deprived of their company or comfort, or that they love someone else more than you."[21] And because these two loves are in fact one inseparable love, our love for others bears the same degree of selfishness as our love for God: "They love their neighbors with the same love with which they love me—for their own profit."[22] In withdrawing our love for another because of selfish reasons, we therefore inescapably diminish also our love for God.[23]

As she counseled others, Catherine grew convinced that a relationship formed outside of God's own charity will produce no true union and "will not endure beyond the pleasure and advantage we draw from it."[24] By loving God "with measure" and another human person "without measure," we replace God's charity with what Catherine calls "selfish sensuality." She pictures self-centeredness as a clever thief creep-

---

[18]D 144, p. 302.

[19]D 60, p. 114.

[20]Let T 38 to Monna Agnesa Malavolti; Scudder, p. 40.

[21]D 64, p. 121.

[22]D 60, p. 114.

[23]Let T 126 to Monna Alessa and Monna Cecca.

[24]Let T 268 to the Elders and Consuls of Bologna; Catherine here warns the leaders of Bologna, joined with Florence in revolt against the Holy See, that their alliances formed apart from charity will in the end betray them.

ing into the "house" of our relationship and gradually steal-
ing away a generous love founded in God. Without realizing
the deceptive process at play, we awake one day to find the
entire house in ruins.[25]

Selfishness in this way makes our life a foretaste of hell,
for we continually suffer either from fear of losing what we
have or from desire for what we want and cannot get.[26]
Instead of loving others "in God," with liberty of heart and
clinging only to God, selfish love relates to others in a grasping, unfree way. "We go on forming attachments," Catherine
writes to Monna Biancina Salimbeni. "If God severs one
branch, we make another."[27] She reminds another person
that when we replace the bond of the Spirit's love with the tie
of selfish love, we gain in place of union only "division and
separation leading to nothing."[28] And to her niece Eugenia
she writes, "Bind your heart to none but Jesus, for the time
will come when you will wish to set it free and you will not
be able to."[29]

When we love with imperfect love, we never have peace,
since even the friend once loved will eventually become
unbearable to us. "They love and possess creatures apart
from me, and so they pass through this life tormented,
becoming insupportable even to themselves."[30] And yet, if
we are open to it, a gift lies hidden in the pain of a selfish
relationship, for God often allows us to "form such a love"
precisely so that we will recognize our own weakness and
our need to grow in the love that only God can give.[31]

[25]Let T 245 to a Genoese man of the third order of St. Francis.

[26]Let T 194 to Monna Tora Gambacorti.

[27]Let T 111.

[28]Let T 164 to Monna Mellina Barbani, from one of Lucca's most powerful
families.

[29]Let T 26 to Eugenia, Catherine's niece.

[30]D 55, p. 110.

[31]D 64, p. 121.

Draw from the Source

Jesus commands us to love one another as he loves us (Jn 13:34). Catherine saw that he allows no qualifications that would add, "If they hurt you, do not love them."[32] The triune God has made us to love as Jesus himself does, unselfishly and "without regard" for our own interest, intimately, with liberty of heart, and for the other's good rather than for our own advantage.[33] Yet even when we appear to love unselfishly, we are often reaching out only to meet our own needs. Catherine herself in this way learned that we gain the gift of unselfish love only by making our home in the inner dwelling of self-knowledge, where we learn our need and God's mercy. She saw that it is God's gracious gift to us even to recognize our failures in loving, since the painful but freeing truth (Jn 8:31) makes us all the more fertile ground to receive God's own power to love.

Catherine saw in prayer that God's heart, a "deep well of charity," has fallen so "madly in love" with us that he seems unable to live without us.[34] The Father fills his every work only with infinitely tender love. If we run away from him he runs to us; the more we sin, the closer he comes to us. The Son clothed himself in our own humanness and "nearer than that" he "could not have come."[35] And although our sin deserved only punishment, the Father found a better way, the most sweet and tender way he could find, for he saw that nothing so triumphs over the human heart as love. Because love alone has brought us into existence, we can be won in no better way than by love;[36] the triune God thus continually "throws out" to us the "bait of love."[37] And when we wonder

[32]D 156, p. 334.

[33]D 60, p. 114.

[34]D 25, p. 63.

[35]D 153, p. 325.

[36]Let T 196 (DT 64) to Pope Gregory XI.

[37]Ibid.

what God loves so much, the Father answers, "Look in yourself and you will find what I love."[38]

"Ask and it will be given you" (Lk 11:9). Catherine's friend Caffarini writes that every day of her life she asked for the gift of perfect love, and she herself continually stressed that God lavishes his gifts on those who desire them. Catherine's experience of the exchange of hearts and her desire for the blood of Jesus—dimensions of her spirituality which could seem exaggerated today—symbolize this truth too deep for words, that we need God's own heart to love unselfishly. While Catherine certainly prayed, "Lord, I give you my heart," even more she prayed, "Lord, give me your heart." And no symbol more concretely or radically expresses the unconditional love of God's heart than the blood poured out from the torn flesh of Jesus.

This is why Catherine invites us to the cross, where we find prayer as the mother of unselfish love. For prayer unites us to the "fire of love," and what is touched by fire becomes fire. She pictures the Lord also as the fountain of living water (Jn 4:14) satisfying the human heart with unbounded love. As long as we love others by drawing from this fountain, our capacity to love will grow rather than diminish; only when we take the vessel of our heart out of the fountain will it become empty. If, however, we hold our heart "in the fountain" while we drink, "it will not get empty; indeed, it will always be full." And because it is no easy thing to love—for our isolation and possessiveness do not die easily—God asks us to drink all of our love of others only in him and "without any self-interest."[39]

When we love others in this way, Catherine writes to Donna Mellina of Lucca, we love them "in God." St Augustine, whose thought greatly influenced Catherine's, explains the meaning of loving others "in God." Reflecting on the passage from the Letter to Philemon, "May my heart be refreshed by your love, and may I enjoy you in the Lord,"

[38]Let T 134 to Bartolomeo and Iacomo, hermits in Pisa.
[39]D 64, pp. 120-121.

Augustine comments that lust clings to created reality without reference to God. Yet since only God's infinite love can fulfill the human ache, our attempts to satisfy our heart with simply created good only bring us more emptiness.

When we love others "in God," therefore, we enjoy their love, not as a permanent resting place, but as comfort and strength given to us as travelers on the way home. In the same way that refreshment enables pilgrims to continue their journey, the joy of another's love is meant to support and sustain us in directing our heart to God. In turn, our loved ones are to be caught up and carried along with us on the journey, so that they, too, may love God with all of their hearts.[40] Any love that cannot be referred to God in this way ultimately becomes, as Thérèse of Lisieux later said, a lie.[41]

Charity, Bond of the Spirit

Like one who swims underwater, the person who loves "in God" sees everything only from within the ocean of God's love. Catherine loved to think of Mary Magdalen whose love made her see the face of Jesus wherever she turned. Heedless of the soldiers or of her reputation, she ran to Jesus' tomb with one purpose in mind, to find and to follow her Lord; for, compared with his love, her former vanities held no appeal for her.[42] Like Magdalen, when we ourselves love "in God," we begin to see everything in the light of his love and "no longer lust after anything outside of God."[43]

Catherine found a symbol of the Holy Spirit, source of all love, in the gentle image of a mother nursing her child. Just

---

[40]St. Augustine, *On Christian Doctrine* 1.33.37; 3.10.16; 1.22.20; *De Trinitate* 9.7.13.

[41]St. Therese of Lisieux, *Her Last Conversations*, translated by John Clarke, O.C.D. (Wa., D.C.: ICS Pubblications, 1977), p. 67.

[42]Let T 165 (DT 59) to Monna Bartolomea di Salvatico da Lucca.

[43]R 1.10, p. 93.

as Jesus feeds us at his breast, the Spirit, our mother,[44] nurses us at God's breast, tenderly feeding us with the milk of God's own unbounded love.[45] Catherine became convinced that, if we learn to taste all of life's experiences in this milk, everything we undergo will hold its own sweetness for us.[46] She pictures charity itself as a mother who nurtures every virtue in us;[47] for, since this mother never rests, charity works for us even as we sleep, making everything profitable for us as we live in love. "Oh charity, full of joy! You are a mother nourishing the virtues as children at your breast. You are rich beyond all wealth, so rich that the soul clothed in you cannot be poor." And because it unites us with beauty itself, charity shines forth from us with a splendor greater than any physical beauty.[48]

In contrast to selfishness, charity so binds us to each other that "what is loved by the one is loved by the other."[49] While selfish love cuts us off from our brothers and sisters, charity expands our heart until we have room within us for the entire world.[50] As Raymond himself recounts, Catherine understood the practical implications of love's expansiveness, for she constantly met Christ "in the person of his poor,"[51] discovering that what she had generously given to the needy she had in fact lavished on Christ himself.[52] She saw that God's own love forbids us to pretend that the poor are not our concern;[53] for, just as every relationship based on

---

[44]D 74, p. 136.

[45]D 141, p. 292.

[46]Let T 165 (DT 59) to Monna Bartolomea de Salvatica da Lucca.

[47]Let T 263 to Monna Montagna.

[48]Let T 108 (DT 49) to Monna Giovanna di Capo and Francesca, in Siena; Noffke, trans.

[49]Let T 101 (DT 23) to Cardinal Iacopo Orsini.

[50]Let T 263 to Monna Montagna.

[51]R 2.3, p. 134.

[52]R 2.3, pp. 129, 132.

[53]Let T 315 to Don Pietro da Milano, Carthusian.

selfishness inevitably dies,[54] so, too, the charity that does not reach out to the poor finally becomes a lie.

Because none of her *famiglia* wanted to be without her presence, Catherine's travels often occasioned jealousy among her disciples. Those fortunate enough to travel with her—and even Catherine herself—in this way became the object at times of gossip in their absence. But we have only to read some of Catherine's letters to those left behind at Siena to feel the force of her commitment to the charity that is "patient and kind" (1 Cor 13:14). Having learned compassion and respect for seemingly unimportant people, charity despises no one, and attends to our own faults and weaknesses rather than to those of our neighbors.[55]

When we live covered and clothed with the Spirit's charity, our love for one another will deepen even in times of difficulty. Catherine's own experience showed her that awareness of our own weakness, and compassion for that of our brothers and sisters, most surely open the path for us to peace and unity. "Every division comes from paying attention to others' faults instead of our own."[56] She saw that patience and mutual forgiveness so strengthen the charity among us that nothing can ultimately divide us, even in our differences.[57] Just as the power of the Spirit's love held the Son of God fastened to the cross, so too this same Holy Spirit binds us together with a love strong and faithful enough to endure. "Clothed in the fire of the Holy Spirit," that garment "so strong and tough that nothing weakens its fiber," we can trust our mutual love to deepen rather than to diminish with time.[58]

---

[54] Let T 164 (DT 58) to Monna Mellina Barbani da Lucca.

[55] Let T 62 to Sano di Maco and others at Siena.

[56] Let T 175 to a monastry of nuns.

[57] Let T 79 to the Abbess and nuns of San Pietro in Monticelli.

[58] Let T 129 (DT 29) to Frate Bartolomeo Dominici, O.P.; Noffke, trans.

Love That Endures

Not even death can separate those whom the Holy Spirit unites, for the bonds of charity not only continue forever but also open to us even now the depth of the communion of saints. Catherine herself promised that she would be of more help to her friends after her death than during her lifetime. And although he had not yet received word of her death, Raymond experienced her, that very day in Genoa, speaking to his heart these words, "Fear absolutely nothing. I am here for you. I am in heaven for you. I will protect you and defend you. Do not be anxious; do not be afraid."[59] Even before her death, Catherine experienced a close communion with two friends whom she had never met on earth, Mary Magdalen and Agnes of Montepulciano.

Catherine's own reflections on the moment of death show how deeply she had been touched by the beauty of the love through which the triune God binds us together. The door of heaven opens to us through the blood of Christ, and like bridesmaids adorned for a wedding, our virtues come with us as far as this door—but then stop at its threshold. Then charity emerges, charity the bride; leaving her attendants at the entrance to the chamber, she alone proceeds into the bridal room. No other virtue enters heaven, because no other is needed here—"not faith, nor hope, nor patience." Like attendant bridesmaids, the other virtues have prepared us for heaven, but charity receives the reward, for the love which alone united us to God on earth now enters into heaven and becomes its very life.[60]

Will the love we have for one another here on earth endure in heaven? Catherine writes that our love now gives us only a taste of the closeness which will be ours forever. For while charity unites us to everyone, we will experience a unique intimacy with those who have been dearest to us on earth: "They know a special kind of sharing with those

[59]R 3.4, p. 342.
[60]Let T 345 to Contessa Giovanna di Mileto.

whom they loved most closely." Having helped one another to live for God on earth, we do not lose our love for one another in heaven. "No, they still love and share with each other even more closely and fully, adding their love to the good of all."[61]

The gladness of those intimately joined on earth will become in this way the delight of all in heaven, for when we reach eternal life, everyone in heaven will share in our joy, and we in theirs. At our arrival, the saints "experience a new freshness in their exultation—a mirthfulness, a jubilation, a gladness" in receiving us into their embrace. And all that the Lord has done for each of us will give deepened cause for praise and exultation to everyone.[62]

The same affection in which we die becomes the closeness in which we live on forever, and our joy expands in proportion to our love. Because charity has joined us to God and to one another, love will cause the joy of one to be the joy of all. We will enter into the triune God's own unspeakable gladness, and God's delight will become ours; in turn, the joy of each one of us will add to the delight of all of us.[63] "There is so much love and mutual charity among them that the smallest does not envy the greatest.... All are content and happy in their mutual joy."[64] The "small" participate in the reward of the "great," and the "great find joy in the reward of the small."[65] Thus the saints eagerly await us at heaven's threshold, holding out to us the arms of their love to beckon us home.

"My nature is fire," Catherine once said,[66] and the one who had claimed her in her entirety was the abyss of that fire. Her words on her deathbed express the word her whole life had spoken, "Love one another." From the God "mad

---

[61]D 41, p. 83.

[62]*Ibid.*

[63]D 148, p. 313.

[64]Let T 345 to Contessa Giovanna di Mileto.

[65]D 148, p. 312.

[66]Pr 12, p. 104.

with love" for us she had learned to embrace with her life the people for whose sake she had been separated from the Lord. Not even death could destroy the bonds the Lord had formed between her and those he had given her. In a prayer dating from the time three months before her death when, as she herself said, the vessel of her body became "all shattered," she prays to the Father, "Bind them together with the gentle chain of charity;...let none of them be snatched from my hands....I offer and commend to you my children, whom I so love, for they are my soul."[67]

The fire and boldness of Jesus' love had become Catherine's. Her heart, vulnerable as a child's, could be comforted by letters and hurt by thoughtlessness; but it was also the heart which she begged Jesus to squeeze out over the face of his hurting and beloved Church. The arms which loved to gather flowers, to caress children, and to embrace her loved ones were the same arms which received the severed head of a man whom her affection had converted to God.

Catherine's love was not weakness. The tenderness of her affection was equaled by its strength; the ardor of her heart, by its purity and freedom. Her heart belonged to one alone, and from this one love, as from a fountain and fire, all her other relationships drew their lifeblood and were borne along with her to that source as to their final goal. When Catherine herself had asked the question of how such love could be gained, the Lord's answer to her became the one she would surely give to us today, for "where two friends have one soul there can be no secret between them." "Love is gained in love, by raising the eye of our mind to behold how much we are beloved of God."[68]

---

[67]Pr 26, p. 226.

[68]Let T 169 to Frate Matteo Tolomei, O.P., and Don Niccolò di Francia; Scudder, p. 80.

8

Trusting in the Providence of God

"Cast all of your anxieties" on the Lord, "for he cares" for you (1 Pet 5:7). In her *Dialogue* Catherine expresses with unique insight a central truth experienced by men and women of faith throughout the ages: far from allowing us to escape the reality of life, a radical trust in God's providence provides the focal point for a key human conversion. We begin to place our trust not simply in our own limited resources and efforts, but in the abundant and intimate providence of God. Paradoxically, the choice to trust radically in God's care opens us to a spirituality capable of nourishing in us authentic personal autonomy and mature interdependence.

Early in Catherine's life the Lord had pledged that he would make her his concern if she would make him her concern. Experience of her helplessness in situations which her efforts proved powerless to change faced Catherine daily with the same choice which in some way confronts every human being: either to trust or to despair. Who of us by being anxious can add a cubit to his or her life? "If then you are not able to do as small a thing as that, why are you anxious about the rest?" Our Father knows our needs. "Seek his kingdom, and these things shall be yours as well" (Lk 12:25-26, 30-31). Toward the end of her life, Catherine reflected on the Lord's fidelity to his promise made in her youth. One result is the section in her *Dialogue* which rings out as a hymn of praise to the infinite mercy of a provident God.[1] Raymond writes that Catherine's insights on the providence of God explicate the very foundation of her spirituality, the experience of the frailty of our own resources, and the absolute power of God's love for us.[2]

The Choice to Trust

In life's most precious experiences we recognize the fruit of trust, the paradox of security in the presence of what we cannot unequivocally verify. Around us are alluring traces of the trust which makes human life possible at all: the vulnerability of a child asleep in a parent's arms; the secret shared between friends; the vow said and then lived, to love faithfully until death. But life leaves also its scars. Those who know betrayal, who neither trust nor are trusted, recognize the fruit of this distrust in a sense of worthlessness which eats away at their identities, in an anxiety and fear which rob them of peace.

In the face of what life has held out to us, a deeper question and choice inevitably confront us in our daily decisions. Has life been ultimately gracious to us, or has it cheated and betrayed us? When we ask this question, we ask the meaning of our past experiences taken as a whole, and what choice we will make to live out the future in light of that meaning.

More than most, Catherine knew what it was to live through the bitterness of life and to have those for whom she had poured out her energies turn against her. And yet she made her choice; for Catherine the entire universe is ruled, not by forces which rob and deceive us, but by the provident mercy of God. She learned to trust that all of creation is made for us and that we are the fragile and precious work

---

[1] D 135-153, pp. 277-326.
[2] R 1.10, p. 91.

with whom God has fallen "madly" in love. God has given us everything with love and care: every facet of creation, every gift and faculty of our unique persons. In every event of history the Father has unfolded his mercy until finally he did not spare even his own Son. We can trust, therefore, that God wants only our good; having provided for our needs in the past, he will not betray us in the future.[3]

Catherine realized that only by making the radical choice to trust in God's providence will we be able to experience its fullness. The God who infinitely respects our freedom will not force his love on us; but, if we place our hope in him, we will discover for ourselves how faithfully his providence cares for us, even in the smallest matters.[4] Yet Catherine emphasizes that this trust cannot exist side by side with a contrary hope in ourselves alone, for then we rely on "what is not." When we trust in God, we let go of depending simply on our own resources and cling to the one "who is." By entrusting ourselves to God's care in this way, we open ourselves to receive the gift hidden in every moment of life.

Yet how can we receive with love and reverence the tragedies which evoke from us only anger and bitterness? Are not experiences of pain and disappointment empty of the providence of God? "On the contrary," the Father tells Catherine. "No matter *where* they turn. . . [those who trust in my providence] will find nothing but my deep burning charity, and the greatest, gentle, true, perfect providence."[5] Even in life's tragedies, God's providence works to bring life from death. Rather than denying or repressing anger in the face of suffering, we are called to work through our pain and to grow in the peace and joy which recognize God's tenderness and care in even the most painful of our experiences.

[3]D 135, p. 278.
[4]D 136, p. 280.
[5]D 141, p. 290.

The Wealth Hidden Within

Catherine's experience taught her that we find particularly bitter the discovery that everything created, despite its goodness, will eventually fail us. In times of loss, we often cry out against the God whose providence seems to have abandoned us and deprived us of what our plans had fashioned. We "lift up our heads against the goodness of God," writes Catherine, and draw death from what was intended to give life because we "do not recognize the wealth within."[6]

How can we discover the "wealth" hidden within our experiences? Seeing how easily we resist inner growth, God's tenderness provides exactly what we need at any given moment. "How can you lift up your head against my goodness?... All things except my grace are changing and...because you...are constantly changing, I am constantly providing for what you need at any given time."[7] We so often cling to present yet outgrown securities that unless someone else removed them from us we would grow little in human maturity. God's tender care in this way allows people and investments to fail us so that in the absence of previous supports our trust in him may lead us to greater personal autonomy.

God thus permits the "wearisome thorns" of life, not out of hatred but out of love for us,[8] so that we gradually and painfully learn that nothing created can be God for us. This collapse of hope in other supports then draws us to the one who will not fail us: "I wanted her to learn that although everyone else might fail her, I her Creator would never fail her...and that with or without the help of another person, in any situation or at any time whatever...I know how to and can and will satisfy her in wonderful ways."[9]

If we place our trust not in ourselves but in God, we

[6]D 141, p. 291.
[7]D 136, p. 282.
[8]D 141, p. 290.
[9]D 142, p. 296.

eventually experience the fruit of this trust. God becomes our provider and gives us the "mercy" of the Holy Spirit to nurse us at the breast of God's love.[10] As the Spirit our mother feeds us with the milk of gratitude and love, our fear and insecurity gradually starve for want of food. Nourished in this way, we become with time strong and confident, able to see life with new eyes in the light given by the Spirit. Slowly we begin to hold "all things in reverence, the left hand as well as the right, trouble as well as consolation." As we learn to cherish the gift hidden within even painful situations, we see God's mercy forming us in greater trust and interior strength.[11]

The "Holy Tricks" of Providence

In order to make us "drunk" with his providence, the Lord devises "holy tricks" perfectly suited to meet our needs at any particular moment. When we are caught fast in sin, God's providence "plucks the rose" from our "thorns." The sin enslaving us becomes the thorn; the rose, the lack of satisfaction we find in that sin. We set our "affection on something...but...find nothing there." By means of the sweeter gift of his peace, God's providence thus entices us away from sin's unfreedom.[12]

In different circumstances, the Lord employs other "holy tricks," finding ways to humble us when we gossip, judge others, or complain and "spit out hurtful words." For our healing, the Lord's tenderness may allow us to experience emptiness and darkness or allow temptations to besiege us. "Why do I keep her in such pain and distress? To show her my providence so she will trust not in herself but me." Humbled through these struggles, we learn the contrast

[10]D 141, p. 291.

[11]D 141, p. 292.

[12]D 143, p. 297.

between our own weakness and the provident love of God for us, for the Lord himself eventually frees us in deeper ways than we could have imagined. Serenity and peace come unforeseen, not through our own efforts, but through the Lord's "immeasurable charity" which provides especially for us in time of need when we can "scarcely take any more."[13] The struggles which humble us are nothing less than God's own gift to us: "The soul comes to perfection by fighting these battles, because there she experiences my divine providence, whereas before this she only believed in it."[14]

If we have been formed in virtue, the Lord provides for us in still other ways by using a "pleasant trick" to keep us humble. Often, after we have borne the weight of burdens and sufferings with patience and gentleness, perhaps for years, God allows us to feel passion or rage at a mere trifle: "In something that really is nothing, that they themselves will later laugh at, their feelings are so aroused that they are stupefied." At other times, God's providence leaves us a "pricking" such as Paul experienced: "I left him...the resistance of his flesh." Is God able to heal our weakness? Certainly, the Father tells Catherine, but his providence leaves us "this or that sort of pricking" so that we will grow humble and "compassionate instead of cruel" to one another. When we suffer from our own weakness, we have cause to be all the more compassionate toward the weakness of others.[15]

The Gentle Physician

Catherine compares God's provident love to the healing remedies of a gentle doctor whose skill ministers to every wound.[16] The God who loved us "before we were made" cannot stop loving us: what God creates once is cherished

---

[13] D 144, p. 301.

[14] D 144, pp. 301-302.

[15] D 145, p. 305.

[16] Let T 13 to Marco Bindo.

forever. And because the Lord will not withdraw the love in which he has created us, love alone enfolds and supports us through every moment of our lives. Each of us requires uniquely tender and resourceful means of healing; and, when pleasant tasting medicines have no effect, God often applies more bitter remedies,[17] not out of hatred, but out of love for us.[18] Like a mother gently removing a destructive object from her child's grasp, the Lord allows people and plans on which we have depended to fail us. But in the same way that unpleasant tasting medicines often contain the most healing cures, God's love can so transform our tragedies that they finally bear only sweetness for us and convey to us nothing but love.[19]

Catherine realized how we recoil in the face of tragedy, as others' evil or carelessness often destroys the lives and property of innocent people. Viewed without faith, these events shout out evidence of a God indifferent to our suffering. Yet Catherine gazed at life with deeper vision. God's ardent love permits the human freedom and natural forces responsible for life's tragedies only because this love is powerful enough to embrace in its arms even senseless evil and to create from chaos the miracle of new life. God's love thus permits every event in our lives not as a way to hand us over to death but to rescue us from true death.

Yet we easily misjudge God's love, distorting and distrusting the divine purpose and care. If we see without faith, trust in God's providence in bitter tragedy appears utterly "unreasonable," for the foolish "take for death" what God permits for life. God's tender love bears patiently with our

[17]Let T 320 to Stefano di Corrado Maconi, a member of a consular family of Siena. Converted by Catherine after he became weary of constant family feuds, he became her secretary and beloved friend, accompanying her on almost every one of her journeys. After Catherine's death, Stefano joined the Carthusians and later became head of that Order.

[18]Let T 48 to Matteo di Giovanni Colombini of Siena. Matteo was related to two saints who were also contemporaries of Catherine: Bl. Giovanni Colombini, founder of the Gesuati, and Bl. Caterina Colombini, foundress of the women's branch of this company.

[19]D 134, p. 274.

complaints, however, and continually enfolds us with the "supreme providence" which those who love have experienced.[20]

A good physician intends to bring us to health and to keep us in good health. Neither task is possible, however, if we put our trust in our own resources, making our own diagnoses and prescribing our own cures. Unlike that of even the best of doctors, God's providence never makes a mistake: the Lord's infinite wisdom and power work from within our being to effect true healing and freedom. But we need to open ourselves to God's care, to want it, and to receive it with all of our heart. If we hesitate to place ourselves into the hands of this provident and gentle physician, we have only to look at those who have made this choice: their lives speak to us of joy and peace, of extravagant and tender care even in the smallest events of life.[21]

Lavish Trust

Like a parent caring for a child or a spouse for the beloved, God continually devises new ways of giving us delight. So infinitely "endless are the ways" of God's care for us that we can never grow used to all of the fresh means God has of surprising us with generous providence and joy.[22] When Catherine herself was deprived of Raymond's presence, the Lord did not leave her bereft; "I asked for you," she writes to Raymond, "and God gave me himself."[23] We cannot imagine how God longs to fill us with all good things, nor how "gently and pleasantly" God gives them. Catherine's own experience of this providence filled her with such gratitude that she could only cry out in praise, "The human heart

---

[20]D 135, p. 277; D 137, p. 283.

[21]D 136, p. 280.

[22]D 143, p. 299.

[23]Let T 226 to Raymond of Capua.

does not so much as know how to desire or ask for all that you give."[24]

Since in the greatest matters—our redemption and healing—the Father has already given the fullest measure of care, he wants us to trust that he works only for our good even in the smallest matters of our daily lives. Catherine recognized that our trust in God's care grows with our love: the more we love, the more we trust, and the more we are open to receive from this love. And while the depth of our hope and trust indicates how much we have let God's love embrace us, even when we love imperfectly, God's providence will never fail us if we but place our trust in him.[25]

Catherine was convinced that the same love which created us continues to enfold us in all that happens in our life.[26] Yet we are often blind to God's care; clinging to our own resources, we prevent ourselves from experiencing the depth of God's providence for us. As we attempt to divide our trust between two "contradictory" directions—God's care and the frailty of created supports—we find ourselves deceived. "Because her hope is set on empty finite passing things, her hope will fail her and she will never in effect attain what she desires."[27]

Unlike God's faithfulness, our trust can be empty and fickle, interpreting our experiences as bereft of God's care when in reality they are filled with love.[28] For although God remains absolutely faithful to us, we often doubt his mercy and power to lavish every good gift upon us.[29] Yet when we depend on created supports, we frequently find ourselves betrayed by the very realities we served.[30] It is then that we discover in contrast how generously God's love embraces

[24]D 134, p. 274.

[25]D 136, p. 281.

[26]D 138, p. 284.

[27]D 136, p. 280.

[28]D 138, p. 284.

[29]D 140, pp. 286-87.

[30]Let T 143 to Giovanna, Queen of Naples.

and upholds us even when we complain, even when we forget that we are infinitely loved without loving in return.[31] And precisely because the "measure of our confidence" sets limits on how much we allow God to provide for us,[32] Catherine urges her disciples to lavish extravagant, unbounded trust upon the Lord who "measures his gifts to our hope."[33]

"Think of Me and I Will Think of You"

Early in her life the Lord invited Catherine to trust him in everything and to make her only concern that of pleasing him and doing his will: "Think of me and I will think of you." She was to give all fear and anxiety to him, concentrating on his love for her rather than on her own or others' weakness. If she would give herself to God's love in every situation instead of dwelling on negative thoughts, nothing would be able to destroy the "even tenor of her taking thought for him."[34]

The Lord promised Catherine that if she trusted him, she would have no reason for anxiety in any physical or spiritual need: "I will think of you." If she made his love her concern, the Lord would make care of her every need his own concern. Catherine in this way began to understand how God's tender love takes thought for us "with watchful care," freeing us from preoccupation with our own needs so that we may attend to his love and be present to others. In trusting God's providence in our life, we thus paradoxically reach the fullness of human maturity: "This for you is perfection; this for you is your final end and goal."[35]

Because baptism has given us over "into the hands of God," we are to have "no anxiety about ourselves," but

---

[31]D 138, p. 285.

[32]Let T 272 to Raymond of Capua.

[33]Let T 85 to Pietro di Tommaso de' Bardi, a governor of Florence.

[34]R 1.10, p. 90.

[35]*Ibid.*

rather to direct our attention to the Lord who has made our every need his concern. Raymond comments that whenever he or others would grow fearful or worried, Catherine would say, "Why must you have such care for yourselves? Let God's providence watch over you. His eyes are on you continually in your fears. Not a moment passes but he is thinking of your welfare."[36]

"Ask and it will be given you" (Lk 11:9). Catherine stresses that we do not gain this kind of trust simply by willing it; God desires to lavish it upon us as his own gracious gift to us. If we ask for trust daily, and direct our thought to God's care rather than to reasons for worry, we will begin to taste an abiding peace in even the most troublesome of situations. In this way we gradually learn to receive all that happens in our life with reverence instead of bitterness and to nurture peace instead of turmoil in our heart.[37] As we discover how God's providence remains more sure than our own existence, we will experience for ourselves how truly God's care never fails or disappoints us.[38]

The mercy of God, the Holy Spirit, wants to so strengthen our dependence on God that our own love will reach out to the needs of the poor among us.[39] Catherine emphasizes that the Spirit's love enlarges our trust so that we will not hold back our heart and hands from charity to the poor:[40] "You ought to be the providence of the poor, of those who have nothing."[41] When we allow the Holy Spirit to possess and lead us, we become in this way not so much "possessors" of wealth as "distributors" of wealth to the poor among us.[42]

Catherine found the most radical trust in God's providence in those who choose to live in simplicity and poverty.

[36]*Ibid.*

[37]Let T 318 to Sano di Maco and others at Siena.

[38]Let T 85 to Pietro di Tommaso de' Bardi of Florence.

[39]D 143, p. 297.

[40]D 141, p. 290.

[41]Let T 304 to Monna Lodovica di Granello.

[42]D 151, p. 319.

The apostle Matthew "leaped up from his tax booth, and leaving his great wealth behind," chose Jesus as his only treasure.[43] Great leaders of the Church, followers in the apostles' footsteps, had no anxiety that either they or their people would lack what they needed, and so they generously distributed the "Church's possessions to the poor." When these ministers died, "there was no great estate to settle," for they had not hoarded riches. Trusting in God's providence and filled with charity for the poor, they were confident that just as they had cared for the poor, God would care for them and "they would lack nothing."[44]

A life lived without fear thus became for Catherine the surest sign of abandonment to God's care. "Those who trust in themselves are afraid of their own shadows; they expect both heaven and earth to let them down." Since trust in our self-sufficiency deprives us of the "companionship" of charity, we often live isolated and afraid "of every little thing." Forgetting who we are and who God is, we live unmindful of God's mercy and care, depending on our own poor resources. And yet, as the Father gently recalls to Catherine, "every effort is useless for those who think that they can guard their city by their own toil or concern, for I alone am the guardian."[45] When our trust in God is "generous," however, no human power can harm us; on the contrary, our very trust will disarm others.[46]

The Chain of Charity

Catherine discovered that our love for one another becomes the most tender means by which the provident God cares for us. The triune God has fashioned us in the image of the trinitarian communion. Made by love itself, we are also

[43] *Ibid.*
[44] D 119, p. 226.
[45] *Ibid.*
[46] *Ibid.*, p. 227.

made for the love that needs and cares for one another. The triune God has so bound us to each other "with the chain of charity" that no person possesses the resources to meet all of his or her own needs. "No, I gave something to one, something else to another, so that each one's need would be a reason to have recourse to the other."[47] Could God have given everyone as an individual all that he or she needs? Yes, the Father tells Catherine, "but in my providence I wanted to make each of you dependent on the others, so that you would be forced to exercise charity."[48]

Thus, for example, the poor who place their trust in God will experience for themselves the providence that cares for them through others. Sometimes those in need are brought "to the brink" only so that they may see all the more clearly the miracle of the Lord's care for them.[49] At times the provident God acts directly, as with Dominic, causing bread to appear for the friars who had nothing to eat. Usually, however, God inspires us to pray for and to come to the aid of the poor ourselves. In many ways God touches and impels us to provide for others in need, so that even those dedicated to solitude cannot escape the chain of charity which binds us to one another.[50] The Lord in this way "stretches out" the arms of his providence to the poor by inspiring us with compassion for our brothers and sisters: "The whole life of my gentle poor is thus cared for by the concern I give the world's servants for them."[51]

Catherine discovered that God meets even our deepest needs through our brothers and sisters. For a "holy trick" of his providence inspires us at times with a "special love" for another, a love that eventually brings to light our insecurity and jealousy, our isolation or possessiveness, our manipulation and selfishness. The inner struggle uncovered through

[47]D 148, p. 311.
[48]*Ibid.*, p. 312.
[49]D 149, p. 314.
[50]D 151, p. 324.
[51]D 149, p. 314.

the pain of such a relationship leads us to humble self-knowledge and dependence on God's healing. And as we grow through trials of this kind into deeper personal autonomy and freedom, "a greater and more perfect love for others in general as well as for the special person" God's goodness has given us will deepen in our life.[52]

God's providence thus inextricably binds itself to our care for one another, since we ourselves become the living sacrament of God's mercy to our brothers and sisters. But as our love grows, we will know both deeper joy and deeper sorrow. Identified with Jesus, we will live out Paul's experience, "It is no longer I who live but Christ lives in me" (Gal 2:20). When we recognize how "ineffably" God loves us, we, too, begin to fall in love with the beauty of the persons redeemed by Christ's blood. Rather than suffering from offenses done to us, we find ourselves grieving over sin against the Lord and the plight of sinners.

Through the chain of charity the Lord provides in a marvelous way at one and the same time for both sinners and those his love inspires to intercede for them. The prayer of others softens the sinner's heart, while those who intercede become themselves more closely united to the Lord through their prayer, as their love and zeal make them "another Christ crucified" who take his task on themselves.[53]

In a charming image, Catherine compares the people whom God's providence unites in love to an orchestra. The Lord, the "maestro," directs us as we play the instrument of our lives, and without every one of us, no single instrument alone suffices. The more sweetly we play our instruments, the more this music allures others to the Lord. Catherine reflects on the "glorious virgin Ursula" and her martyred companions. "She played her instrument so sweetly she caught eleven thousand from the virgins alone." In the same way, the Lord intends the entire orchestra to grow more lovely in its sound, swelling to make music filling heaven and

[52]D 144, p. 303.
[53]D 145, p. 306.

earth with its praise. For as we trust in God, we learn to receive everything that happens to us as a gift refining our instrument and rendering the music we play with our life more beautiful. God's infinite providence thus cares for us individually and all together, teaching each of us with utterly personal care what and how to play.[54]

A Life of Trust

So tender and faithful is God's providence to us that not even death can loosen the chain of charity by which he binds us to one another. The life of heaven brings us into the joy not only of God but also of our brothers and sisters, and our very delight in one another resounds as a continual praise of God's providence. God has so "ordered our charity that no one simply enjoys his or her reward in this blessed life that is my gift without its being shared by the others." The joy of all adds to the joy of each, and the gladness of each becomes the gladness of all.[55]

When we live in trust, we experience on earth a foretaste of heaven, knowing a joy and peace more secure than what human mis-steps and failures can destroy. The one who trusts learns in this way to rejoice "in what she sees and experiences in herself and others;" glad because of God's goodness to her, she learns to rejoice without jealousy in the goodness of God to others also. She "is not afraid that she will lack the lesser things because by the light of faith she is guaranteed the greater things."[56]

Living in trust brings us to death itself without fear, for the same arms of God's love which held us fast during our lifetime will not loosen their embrace at our death. And because we come to death empty-handed, just as we came to life with nothing as our own, our own works and merits will

[54]D 147, p. 311.
[55]D 148, p. 312.
[56]D 141, p. 293.

not open heaven's doors to us, but only the infinitely provident mercy of God. The Father thus urges us to gaze not at our own weakness and sin, but at his infinite mercy and compassion.[57]

The Father uses the "gentle trick" of drawing us to trust him in every situation of our lives so that we will trust him at this final moment of death.[58] Confiding in no merit of ours, we are to make one last infinitely generous act of trust, lavishing on God the one thing that we have to give him in spite of our sin: absolute trust in his mercy. We are to draw courage from the memory of how faithful God has been to us, never once failing to care for our needs. "In everything they sweetly experience the depth of my providence;" tasting in it the milk of divine tenderness, they do not fear death[59] but instead long for it.[60]

When we trust in God's providence and not in our own resources, we begin to live in peace and contentment, facing death without fear. Realizing that we have nothing to bring to God at this moment, no work or accomplishment, no virtue or grace that is not already God's own gift to us, we lavish upon God the one gift he wants from us, radical trust in his mercy. Having lived in hope, trusting in God and not at all in ourselves, we fashion this same hope and trust into the arms with which we reach out unreservedly to embrace God's mercy at the moment of death.[61]

Catherine's own experience taught her that, far from constituting a "pious exercise," trusting in God's providence forms the entire content of a life lived in love; for the more generous our hope and trust, the more lavish our experience of God's intimate care for us. Yet because this kind of trust exceeds what mere human willing can attain, we learn to ask for it as the gift the provident God most deeply wants to bestow on us. Catherine herself learned that a good memory

[57] D 132, p. 268.
[58] D 132, pp. 267-68.
[59] D 151, p. 322.
[60] D 84, p. 154.
[61] D 131, p. 265.

nourishes trust; for, in reflecting upon the experiences of our own life, we find there the indisputable evidence of God's unfailing care for us. In this way , our own life story becomes our inspiration and encouragement to ask for even greater trust in the future.

Far from masking imprudence or immaturity, this kind of abandonment to God frees us to grow in personal autonomy and mature interdependence. Because it entails the paradox of a radical inner poverty and an equally radical inner contentment, trust ultimately has the heart to let go. Catherine's own dependence on the God who alone is Lord over all invites us to the same unconditional trust that will perhaps speak the most radical statement a contemporary world will hear.

On her death bed, Catherine told her friends that her only task her whole life long had been to "hold on" and never to let go of "unshakable hope and trust in the providence of God." She urged her companions to do the same, assuring them that there exist "no limits of any kind to the providence of God." Catherine invites us today to discover in our own lives the care she herself experienced so intimately. "Never does God's providence fail any who put their trust in it; but in a special way it will be ever careful of yourselves."[62]

[62]R 3.4, p. 336.

9

Trinity, Abyss of Love

"Your face, Lord, I seek. Hide not your face from me" (Ps 27:8-9). As she increasingly trusted the divine providence for her life, Catherine inevitably came face to face with the very mystery of God. She discovered that self-revelation is not wrested from God but bestowed as sheer gift, and it was for this gift that she yearned. Yet the more deeply she lived in the interior dwelling, the more surely she recognized her thirst for God as God's own thirst to give himself to her. The God who unveiled himself to Catherine was not a faceless pit of emptiness, but the one whom Abraham longed to see and did not, the God whom Jesus discloses as the tri-personal intimacy of Father, Son, and Spirit. In the unspeakable joy and nearness of this trinitarian communion she discovered, not only her own identity and meaning, but that of the entire universe.

"Let Us Make Humankind in Our Image and Likeness" (Gen 1:26)

Catherine began to ponder the mystery of human creation as it unfolds in the first chapter of Genesis. We who live have been known and loved into life;[1] our very being proves how irrevocably God cherishes us, for we exist only because we are loved. "You saw me and knew me in yourself," she cries out in prayer; "You fell in love with your creature and drew her out of yourself."[2] Catherine heard in her own heart God's word to Jeremiah: "Before I formed you in the womb I knew you" (Jer 1:5). The one whom God intimately "knows" God also loves and draws into life by this love.

The first chapter of Genesis unveiled to Catherine the mystery of our human identity, for in this passage she saw that each one of us has been known and treasured before the universe itself existed. Since we have been loved into being in the "image and likeness" of the Trinity, the womb out of which God has drawn us is not a void of nothingness but the very abyss of the divine heart. As Catherine pondered this mystery, she recognized that she would know her true self only in God and as the reflection of God's love. "In your nature, eternal Godhead, I shall come to know my nature. And what is my nature, boundless love? It is fire, because you are nothing but a fire of love. And... by the fire of love you created us."[3]

"Let us make" humankind "in our image, after our likeness" (Gen 1:26). The contrast between these words and those attributed to the creation of everything else struck Catherine with particular force. The impersonal nature of the refrain, "Let it be made," gave for her added meaning to the mysterious divine cry, let "us" make humankind. The triune God creates all of the universe but celebrates the life of human beings with unique joy. Catherine heard in Genesis 1:26 intimations of the mysterious plenitude of God revealed in Jesus; for the cry, let "us" make humankind, speaks to each of us the story of his or her own unique creation as the gift of the triune God's love and assent.[4]

[1]Pr 18, p. 159.

[2]Pr 12, p. 108.

[3]Pr 12, p. 104.

[4]Pr 1, p. 16.

As she pondered Genesis 1:26, Catherine found her own identity and meaning in the mystery of God's fullness. Jesus reveals God's life as the plenitude of community, the unspeakably personal intimacy of the Father, Son, and Holy Spirit. As from a "matchless garden," the Trinity has drawn forth from their own fullness the lavish beauty of the universe and of every human person. Like a precious flower, each one of us has been enclosed and nurtured in the priceless garden of the triune God's breast. And this creative act of the Trinity does not cease; the Father, Son, and Spirit's love continues to hold in existence what they have drawn forth from themselves. Enclosed in the extravagant love of the Trinity "like the fish in the sea and the sea in the fish," each of us ceaselessly draws life from this trinitarian fullness.[5]

With Augustine, Catherine began to discover in the powers of her own soul a reflection of the Trinity who had fashioned her. The Father who holds and keeps all of creation in his embrace mirrors the mystery of his own identity in the human power of remembering, while the Son, living image and Word of the Father, traces the uniqueness of his person in our capacity for understanding. The Spirit, personal union of the Father and Son, images himself in our human ability to love. Even more deeply, the Trinity desires that we participate at the very core of our being in their own fullness. Our ability to remember shares in a created way in the Father's power, just as our capacity to know and to understand shares in the wisdom of the Son; so, too, the power of our will to love what we know participates in the love and mercy of the Holy Spirit.[6]

Catherine's friends often heard her pray to the God she adored as Trinity. As she saw herself in the resplendent depths of the triune God, she came to know herself as a living image and sacrament of the Father, Son, and Holy Spirit. Realizing that she participated in the Father's power

[5]Pr 20, pp. 187-88.
[6]D 13, p. 29; D 119, p. 222.

through her remembering, in the Son's wisdom through her understanding, and in the Spirit's love through her willing, she gave voice in her prayer to the familiarity and intimacy she experienced with the triune God. She would beg the Father for his faithful strength in her own weakness and in the Church's frailty and sin, and plead with Jesus for light to see and to live the truth with burning clarity. She would raise the cries of her heart to the Spirit for his tender mercy, for the "fire and deep well" of the love that alone held Jesus nailed to the cross.[7]

Jesus himself has unveiled to us a triune God infinitely humble and inviting, unspeakably reverent toward human creation. Catherine plumbed the depths of this truth in an image of the Trinity as our table, food, and waiter. Our infinitely gentle Father is the "table that offers;" his power does not oppress or control, nor does it manipulate or abuse us. Like a table that reverently waits and offers, the gentleness of his love invites all to approach, to come close and to taste willingly. He himself is the living table spread open, defenseless and unthreatening, full of rich fare, for he holds "the most exquisite of foods," his Son Jesus. As the Passover table held for the Hebrews the body of the slain lamb, the living table of the Father gently bears and offers to his children the food of the Lamb, his only begotten Son, to satisfy their hunger and thirst. And the Holy Spirit selflessly ministers to the needs of those at table as humble servant and waiter, offering them the fire of God's own charity as the dish especially his own.[8]

This image of the Trinity as our table, food, and waiter opened Catherine to the height and depth of the paradox at the heart of God. The divine persons burn as an infinite fire of love engulfing the universe with light. The Father, Son, and Spirit, themselves a boundless ocean of peace, feed the entire universe with peace. And in the divine persons, as in a pure translucent crystal, each of us, fashioned in the image

[7]Pr 5, p. 48.
[8]Pr 12, p. 102.

and likeness of God, can see and find his or her own beauty. Even more wonderfully, the divine persons, "mad" with love for us, have devised a way, not only to image themselves in us, but also to image us in themselves. Looking into the mirror of the Trinity, Catherine saw herself. But as she gazed, she saw God in herself, in all of humanity, irrevocably joined and united through the Incarnation of the Son. "I see you fashioned after us and us after you through the union you have effected with humanity....O abyss!...O deep sea! What more could you have given me than the gift of your very self?"[9]

"The Word Became Flesh" (Jn 1:14)

The face of Jesus has unveiled to us the mystery at which we could scarcely guess. The great exaltedness of God has stooped down "to the very lowliness of our humanity's clay" and has revealed in this clay the very mystery of God. "So I with my littleness would be able to see your greatness you made yourself a little one, wrapping up the greatness of your Godhead in the littleness of our humanity....I have come to know you, deep well of charity, within myself, in this Word."[10]

We who have been known and loved before we existed have been drawn forth from the Trinity only through love. But even more marvelously, love has impelled the triune God to share with us the very mystery of the divine inner life. "The Word became flesh and dwelt among us.... And from his fullness have we all received" (Jn 1:14, 16). Jesus has joined us through grace to the very life of the Trinity. The light of divinity now radiates with the color of humanity, for the heat and fire of the Holy Spirit have kneaded the person of the Son into the dough of our humanity.[11] In Jesus, God

[9]Pr 11, p. 90.
[10]Pr 13, p. 109.
[11]D 110, p. 206.

and humankind are made irrevocably one. Shutting himself up in the "pouch" of our humanity, the Son showed that, after the lavishness of our creation, there was nothing left to give us except the very self of God. Truly can the Father, Son, and Spirit ask what more they could have done to make us share and be glad in them.[12]

It was not simply love, but love for us precisely in our weakness and sin, that drew the triune God to us. The Trinity acted as if they were "drunk with love," madly "infatuated" with their creation. In order to rescue us as we lay withered like a fruitless tree cut off from its own life, the triune God engrafted divinity into our humanity's dead tree. "O sweet tender engrafting, you sweetness itself stooped to join yourself with our bitterness.... What drove you? ...Only love.... And was this enough? No, you eternal Word watered this tree with your own blood."[13]

Elisha had raised to life a dead child by laying himself over the boy's lifeless body. Catherine saw in this image the deeper figure of the Son prostrating himself over the dead body of our human race, joining himself to this body member for member, uniting the life of God with the death of humanity. The Son has become flesh, and in him the entire Trinity has come close to us. In the person of Jesus, "all of me, God, the abyss of the Trinity, laid upon and united with your human nature."[14] Catherine names this generous love a "madness" that delights in the one loved as if God were drunk for her salvation. "She runs away from you and you go looking for her. She strays and you draw closer to her. You clothed yourself in our humanity, and nearer than that you could not have come."[15]

Like parents who impart to their children their own nature, Jesus has given to us his divinity, so that we who are

[12]Pr 18, pp. 159-60.
[13]Pr 17, p. 148.
[14]D 140, p. 289.
[15]D 153, p. 325.

powerless could become strong.[16] He has gently tended our wounds and has himself drunk the bitter medicine which our weakness could not endure. In the same way that a wet nurse drinks what is bitter so that the child may get well, Jesus has drunk for us the excruciating cup of death on the cross. "He did as the wet nurse who herself drinks the medicine the baby needs, because she is big and strong and the baby is too weak to stand the bitterness. My Son was your wet nurse."[17]

Jesus loves and cares for us not only as our wet nurse but also as our true mother. The Father invites us to cling to the breast of Jesus as to our mother who feeds us with her own milk. "As an infant when quieted rests on its mother's breast, takes her nipple, and drinks her milk through her flesh. . .so the soul rests on the breast of Christ crucified who is my love, and so drinks in the milk of virtue."[18] And because we drink the very strength of the Father's love at the breast of Jesus, the Lord's milk becomes true meat to feed and strengthen us.[19]

"No one can come to the Father except through me" (Jn 14:6). Catherine realized that we find the Father's own tenderness by feeding at the breast of Jesus crucified, who alone unveils and imparts to us the mysteries of both divine and human life.[20] Because he has entered in his flesh into the depths of our human suffering, the breast of Jesus surges with living water as a fountain at which all can drink (Jn 7:27). His human body has become the living bridge uniting heaven with earth and opening us to the Father's abyss.[21] And because his cross alone bestows on us true life, no one gains access to the Father without entering through the humanity of Jesus.[22]

---

[16]Pr 16, p. 142.

[17]D 14, p. 52.

[18]D 96, p. 179.

[19]D 72, p. 143.

[20]D 96, p. 180.

[21]D 53, p. 106.

[22]D 75, p. 137.

The Son has joined himself irrevocably to all that is human, containing within his own person the treasures of both divinity and humanity, and so has found a way to slake fully our human thirst. Whatever we want to love, whatever we desire of goodness and truth, we find in Jesus. If we want to love what is God, Jesus is God; if we desire to love what is human, he is human. Jesus is Lord, and friend, and brother, the fullness of every treasure sought by the human heart.[23] As Catherine lived in the intimacy of this truth, she learned the profound meaning of the Father's word to her, "Let your place of refuge be my only begotten Son, Christ crucified. Make your home and hiding place in the cavern of his open side."[24]

Raymond recounts how, in the midst of her pressing responsibilities, Catherine grew to experience Jesus as her closest friend, living with him every part of her day. As Catherine herself said, very dear friends share the secrets of their hearts with one another; their affection makes them "two bodies with one soul," so that they keep nothing hidden from each other.[25] And as Catherine shared her life with Jesus, he shared his life with her, opening to her the secrets of his heart.

Jesus unveiled to Catherine the mystery of his union and intimacy with his Father, "The Father and I are one" (Jn 10:30). She saw that the Father, whose glory radiates with beauty infinitely beyond our capacity to know, has drawn utterly near to us in Jesus. "I who am invisible made myself, as it were, visible by giving you the Word, my Son, veiled in your humanity. He showed me to you." In heaven, the Father reveals the mystery of his transcendence to those whose human bodies are "absorbed and filled to bursting in the humanity of the Word,"[26] and even now, the Father manifests himself in the human face of his Son. As she came

[23]Pr 1, p. 18.

[24]D 124, p. 239.

[25]D 60, pp. 115-16.

[26]D 62, p. 117.

close to Jesus and found in him all that the human heart can desire, Catherine discovered also the unspeakable closeness of the Father to her.

"The One Who Sees Me Sees the Father"
(Jn 14:9-10)

The *Dialogue* takes place between Catherine, his "dearest daughter," and the one whom Jesus taught his disciples to call *Abba*—"Daddy," the one who was "most gentle Father" to Catherine. In knowing the intimate friendship of Jesus, Catherine received his Father as her own Father. In reflecting on the lavish effects of the Father's intimacy with us, Catherine thought of Paul's inner strength and security. Paul knew the one who was his origin and final goal, and thus he knew the source of his own identity. Because he experienced his Father's closeness to him, Paul knew from where he had come and where he was going, and so was free to live the truth of his own autonomy and identity in its fullness.[27]

Catherine describes the Father's intimacy with us in images drawn from her own experience of the Father's closeness. As our memories hold and keep within themselves what we know and love, so too the Father holds and cherishes all of creation within himself.[28] Because what the Father would cease to love would cease to exist, he protects all that he has made in his tender embrace.[29] His love burns with extraordinary, boundless fire, for what other father would give up his only child to death in order to ransom a slave?[30] Not only does he provide for the needs of his children with unimaginable love, but he even gives his own Son to the creation at war with him, and sends him as

[27]Pr 4, p. 43.
[28]Pr 1, p. 16.
[29]D 82, p. 152.
[30]Pr 15, p. 133.

a doctor to heal their sickness.[31] Gently he washes his children with the blood of his Son and brightens their faces with the Spirit's gladness.[32]

As she grew to recognize her Father's absolute closeness, Catherine realized that she could run to his embrace in any situation whatever and there find shelter not only for herself but also for the entire world.[33] She experienced the Father revealed by Jesus as the one who covers over his children's faults with unspeakable mercy; when we turn to his embrace in sorrow, we find a Father who cannot remember that we ever sinned.[34] The force by which he rules the world is the strength only of love and infinite mercy; for his mercy alone creates us and holds us in his arms, his mercy alone preserves and defends us, protects and cares for us.[35] And even in tragedy, the Father reveals his own tender face in the blood of his Son, for as we gaze at the wounds of Jesus we discover that the one who looks upon him finds the heart of the Father (Jn 14:9-10).

"You Know the Spirit, For He is With You, and In You" (Jn 14:16-17)

As Catherine pondered the Gospel of John, she realized that the Father and Son could not be without their Spirit whom Jesus promised to be with and in those who love him. Paul identifies this Spirit as the one through whom God's love has been poured into our hearts (Rom 5:5). With Augustine, Bernard, and Aquinas, Catherine interpreted this passage as an intimation of the Spirit's personal identity. Through her own experience of love, she grew to know the Spirit as the very love of the Father and Son, their

---

[31]D 97, p. 182; D 134, p. 274.

[32]Pr 8, p. 65.

[33]D 108, p. 202.

[34]D 30, p. 71.

[35]D 144, p. 301.

personal union and embrace, their kiss and sigh of love. She saw that when we love, we ourselves participate in a created way in the Spirit who is the "loving charity" of the Father and Son: "I gave her a share in this love, which is the Holy Spirit within her.[36]

Catherine recognized the Holy Spirit not only as the "burning charity" of God, but also as the very person of mercy, the largesse and kindness that reaches down to human weakness with a love gone mad with excess. To our fear and selfish love the Spirit brings the fire of God's own charity, a love so profound and free that those touched and inflamed by it participate in the very abyss of the trinitarian life. The Spirit's fire gently heals our disordered desires, and, like dew, waters what is sterile in our hearts, giving us renewed desire for God. The Spirit's warmth and life extend to all of creation, for we who have known the Spirit's mercy must become inevitably a sacrament of mercy to others.[37]

A paradox burns at the heart of God: the love that rules the universe is love that serves. Catherine recalls the poignancy of Jn 13:4-5: "Having loved his own who were in the world, he loved them to the end. . . . He rose from supper . . .and began to wash his disciples' feet. . . . " Jesus' life had spoken this word to his followers long before the Last Supper; their Lord and master had been in their midst as one who served them (Lk 22:27). Filled with this Gospel imagery, Catherine pictures the Father as our table, the Son as our food, and the Spirit as the one who tenderly waits on us. Though Lord and Giver of life, the Spirit becomes our servant and slave, humbly attending to every need of those who desire and seek him.

When Catherine speaks of the Holy Spirit as servant and waiter, her words recall the parable of Lk 12:35-8: "Happy those servants whom the master finds awake when he comes; . . .he will put on an apron, sit them down at table and wait on them." Jesus unveils to us the unspeakable love

<hr/>

[36]D 74, p. 136.
[37]D 29, p. 70.

of the Trinity, a love whose power submits itself to our weakness so that love may draw forth the free response of love. Catherine applies this image of servant to the Holy Spirit, person of love. The Lord of creation bows down to creation: "The Holy Spirit becomes the server. In his infinite love he is not content that we should be served by others. He wishes to serve us himself."[38] Catherine confides to her friend Tommaso dalla Fonte that her own experience had opened her to this image. On the feast of St. Lucy's martyrdom she found herself mystically seated at the table of the Lamb and in prayer she heard the Lord say to her, "I am the table and the food." The Holy Spirit, however, did not simply serve her this food; the Spirit himself fed her.[39]

Catherine pictures the Holy Spirit ministering to us as tenderly as a mother feeding her child, not only with her own hand, but also with her own breast. As we cling in trust to God, we begin to experience God's care in a unique way: "Such a soul has the Holy Spirit as a mother who nurses her at the breast of divine charity.... The Holy Spirit, whom I in my providence have given her, clothes her, nurtures her, inebriates her with tenderness and the greatest wealth."[40] Most especially, the poor held close to the breast of God drink the "milk of great consolation," for the Holy Spirit nurses "their souls and their little bodies in every situation."[41]

The Spirit, tender mercy of God, lives also with and among us as the powerful strength of God. Catherine's prayer to the Spirit often pleaded for the strength of the Spirit's love whose attraction works "mightily and sweetly": "O Holy Spirit, come into my heart; by your power draw it to yourself."[42] She begged the Spirit's fire to consume selfish love within her and within Church leaders, and to fill them

---

[38] Let T 52 to Frate Jeronimo da Siena, hermit of St. Augustine.

[39] Let T 283 (DT 47) to Tommaso dalla Fonte, O.P.

[40] D 141, p. 292.

[41] D 151, p. 323.

[42] Pr 6, p. 54.

with a blazing love and desire for the Church's reform.[43]
And she longed for the Spirit to pour out upon her and the
whole Church the fire and dew which had so transformed
the apostles, making them fearless in speaking the truth
(Jn 15: 26-7).[44]

Luke identifies the Holy Spirit as the plenitude of the
Father's blessings (Lk 11:13). As Catherine pondered this
mystery, she began to experience the person of the Spirit as
the full treasure of God's heart. Since the Holy Spirit comes
to us with the power of the Father and the wisdom of the
Son, our prayer for the Spirit's activity in our lives increasingly opens us to receive every good gift "in the fullness of
the Holy Spirit." When the Spirit comes close to us, the
entire Trinity draws near, for the Spirit proceeding from the
Father and Son is never without them. It is the Spirit, then,
who brings to us the whole treasure of God, and who dwells
in our hearts and abides on our lips to proclaim the truth.[45]

"I Have Called You Friends" (Jn 15:15)

Catherine was convinced that the intimate experience of
the Trinity in our lives is the gift Jesus longs to bestow on
each of us as our baptismal heritage. Friends give to one
another the gift of intimacy, and Jesus calls us his friends (Jn
15:15). Catherine herself "tasted" the Trinity's closeness as a
result of her deepening friendship with Jesus, who promised
that he and his Father would dwell intimately with those
who love him (Jn 14:21, 23).

Catherine's own experience had shown her the simple
path to this intimacy with the triune God: we are to ask for it
continually as a gift, for the three divine persons make themselves known to us in proportion to our desire for them.

---

[43]Pr 7, p. 59.

[44]Pr 7, p. 60.

[45]D 26, p. 77.

"Sometimes they seek me in prayer," the Father says to Catherine, "wanting to know my power and I will satisfy them by letting them taste and feel my strength." At other times we seek the wisdom of the Son and find our fill as he comes close to us. At still other times we seek God "in the mercy of the Holy Spirit," and the Father's goodness lets us "taste the fire of divine charity."[46] In this way we begin to make the triune God our dwelling place and home, just as the three divine persons have made their home with us.[47] Wherever we turn, we find the Trinity's presence, and in the smallest matters we see intimate signs of the Father's gentle power, the Son's loving wisdom, and the Spirit's tender mercy.[48]

Raymond tells of Catherine's insatiable desire for the Eucharist, and her gratitude that he never prevented her from its frequent reception. In her union with Jesus after Holy Communion she frequently "tasted the depths of the Trinity,"[49] her soul entering into God like the sea in the fish and the fish in the sea.[50] The Eucharist which plunged her into the depths of God, the "sea of peace," imparted to her the grace of increasing intimacy with the entire Trinity. Yet she felt unworthy of so great a gift. Jesus acknowledged that she was indeed unworthy to receive him; "But I am worthy that you should enter into me." Catherine so treasured this word of Jesus to her that she made it her frequent counsel to others who hesitated to receive the Eucharist because of a sense of unworthiness.

Catherine realized that we receive the "whole of God" when Jesus gives himself to us as food.[51] Long after we have received the sacrament of the Eucharist, its effects remain, leaving the imprint of the Trinity's grace and presence in us

[46]D 61, p. 116.
[47]Pr 10, p. 81.
[48]Pr 12, p. 100.
[49]D 111, p. 210.
[50]R 1.6, p. 183; D 2, p. 27.
[51]Pr 10, p. 78.

like the seal whose mark is engraved in warm wax. We are
joined with the body and blood of the risen Lord, but in him
we are also united with the Father and the Holy Spirit. The
power of the Eucharist in this way imparts to us the effects
of the entire Trinity's presence: the warmth and light of the
Spirit, the light and wisdom of the Son, and the power and
strength of the Father.[52]

"May They Be One in Us" (Jn 17:21)

The intimate union with the Trinity which Catherine
experienced through the Eucharist so permeated her life that
she desired to live in this closeness continually. She had
found the Trinity imaged in the three powers of her soul; yet
she desired not only to image the Trinity but also to be
united with the triune God within her. "As we image, so may
we find union." In our memories, we are called both to
image and to experience union with the Father's power, just
as through our intellects we image and gain union with the
Son to whom we attribute wisdom. And through our wills
we reflect and grow in union with the Holy Spirit to whom
we attribute love and mercy.[53]

Catherine realized how deeply Paul had united his own
powers of remembering, understanding, and loving with the
three divine Persons. Paul joined his memory with the
Father, whom he knew as his true origin; he made his understanding one with the Son whose wisdom filled him, and he
united his will with the Spirit whose love penetrated him
with gladness.[54] Drawn into the ecstasy of this union, Paul
knew the fullness of the Holy Spirit and so tasted the very
depths of the Trinity.[55] As she reflected on Paul's experience,
Catherine surely desired to fill the powers of her own soul

[52]D 112, p. 211.
[53]Pr 4, p. 42.
[54]Pr 4, p. 43.
[55]D 83, p. 152.

with the Trinity. The Father's words to her could only deepen her thirst for this gift: "If anyone should ask me what this soul is, I would say: "She is another me, made so by the union of love."⁵⁶

The triune God with whom she was united through the effects of the Eucharist joined her in turn to her brothers and sisters. As the Trinity, "all of God," came to her through the body and blood of Jesus, so, too, did "all of humanity." Catherine began to ask Jesus to communicate to her not only himself but also the "mystic body of holy Church and the universal body of Christianity."⁵⁷ Her union with the Trinity began to plunge her so deeply into the divine love for us that her mystical prayer increasingly opened and impelled her outward in ministry to her brothers and sisters. God's love makes the human heart "big, not stingy," she writes, "so big that it has room in its loving charity for everyone."⁵⁸

In Mary, Catherine found an exemplar for the union with the triune God and with one another that Jesus desires for each one of us. Mary lived as the "temple of the Trinity" and "bearer of the Fire;" her very life opens as a book in which we can read God's wisdom, for in her our own "human strength and freedom are revealed." Since the Word came to her with his Father and the Holy Spirit, we see in Mary the reality of the Trinity which the hand of the Holy Spirit has written in her being. Because of her "yes," all of us have gained access to the very life of the triune God given in Jesus. "My soul," Catherine cries out in prayer, "God has become your relative in Mary ."⁵⁹

This sense of wonder and gratitude before the mystery of the triune God's love for us inspired Catherine's most profound outbursts of praise. That the Father, Son, and Holy Spirit would make their dwelling place with the human crea-

---

⁵⁶D 96, p. 181.

⁵⁷Pr 13, p. 108.

⁵⁸Pr 15, p. 131.

⁵⁹Pr 18, p. 162.

tion they have authored,[60] that they would be content only with our intimate sharing in their own life: this was the mystery before which she could only adore. "O God eternal! O boundless love! Your creatures have been wholly kneaded into you and you into us."[61] The profound union of the closest of friends, a union so total that each one's treasure is the other's: Catherine's experience of the Trinity burned with the fire of this intimacy. "O depth of love! What heart could keep from breaking at the sight of your greatness descending to the lowliness of our humanity! We are your image, and now by making yourself one with us you have become our image... You, God, became human and we have been made divine!"[62] Far from being a theoretical and arid doctrine for Catherine, the mystery of the Trinity beame increasingly the deep sea into which she entered with all the powers of her being. The more she entered, the more she discovered and sought. Here, in the depths of the trinitarian life, Catherine discovered the abyss of love infinite enough to satisfy our thirst and to reveal our own deepest meaning: in Jesus, the triune God and humanity have become one.

---

[60]Pr 10, p. 81.

[61]Pr 14, p. 122.

[62]D 13, p. 50.

10

Zeal for Your House Consumes Me

The triune God Catherine came to know was not to be encountered in isolation, for the Holy Spirit drew her out of solitude into passionate engagement with the Church called to express the triune life. Yet the Church of Catherine's time presented itself less as a sacrament of the Trinity's love than as an institution broken by pride and division, a stumbling block and source of scandal to the world. Catherine did not walk away. The secret she saw exposed on the cross took hold of her and began to focus the energies of her life: "Turn yourself to see what God loves so much."[1]

The force of the Trinity's love for the Church Catherine identified as "madness;" yet it was this madness she desired as her own. Having discovered in the Church the living flesh of her Savior, she could not separate her thirst for the world's salvation from the Church so loved by Jesus even in its sin.[2] She reached with the arms of her love deeper than the Church's defects into its inmost heart and there gave herself for her wounded brothers and sisters. This Church

[1]Let T 57 to Matteo Cenni, rector of the Casa della Misericordia in Siena.

[2]Let T 55 to Don William, prior general of the Carthusians.

precisely as she found it—unfaithful spouse and yet true body of the living Lord—she chose to embrace with the unreserved passion of her life and prayer.

At the Heart of the Church

As an adolescent, Catherine had chosen solitude as the path leading her to God; having "turned her back on human companionship," she resolved never to be "enmeshed again in human trammels."[3] When the Lord asked her to open her heart and life to others, therefore, it required of her a conversion of inestimable cost. The young girl who thought she could find God only by separation from the world had to grow into the woman who would find God at the very heart of the world.

Under the Holy Spirit's leading, Catherine began to adopt a radically different way of life; love impelled her to break free of the customary "restraints imposed upon women" of her time, and her solitude gradually gave way to a burning zeal in ministering to others.[4] The people converted to the Lord by the power of her preaching gradually became for her, as they had been for Paul, her "boast, and crown, and joy" (1 Th 2:19).[5] The young girl who before would barely speak with her own family members emerged as a woman boldly preaching and laboring even for a crusade; captivated by the fire of God's love for the world, she could not help wanting the whole world to love him in return.

Like a mother who yearns over the sons and daughters of her womb, Catherine loved and labored for her people "with tears and groans": "And I will give birth...until death as God will give me the grace."[6] No slander or ingratitude intimidated her: "I would sacrifice myself a thousand times if

---

[3] R 2.1, p. 115.

[4] R 2.5, p. 159.

[5] R 2.6, p. 205.

[6] Let T 126 to Monna Alessa and Cecca.

I had the lives...I *will* go and I *will* do as the Holy Spirit inspires me."[7] She writes to a friend that love makes us one with the weakest among us and enlarges us with mercy, for the wounds of the entire world are meant to find in us the infinite mercy of God.[8] Among people unfaithful and ungrateful, cut off from God and from one another, Catherine found her lot.

Grace had broken open her heart, making room in it for her brothers and sisters; like Jeremiah and Paul, she had been lured into giving her life for her people. With Moses and Paul she learned love's boldness, threatening and cajoling the God who inspired in her the divine passion for the world's healing. In this way, Catherine's intercession gradually became less a plea and more the demand of love: she would not "move a foot" from her place of prayer until God granted the mercy she asked for others.[9] Prayer so opened her eyes to the beauty of her people that when her labors seemed fruitless the Lord would encourage her with the thought of the increased radiance of those won back through her effort.[10]

Yet it was far from visible radiance which colored the Church of Catherine's time: "All look only for their own interests and the world's honors and riches—and it is a great poverty."[11] In her *Dialogue* she paints a graphic picture of the priests and Church leaders of her time. "Bloated with pride," they devour money meant for the poor and spend it on their own pleasures. "Woe, woe to their wretched lives!" What the "gentle Word" gained on the cross these priests "spend on prostitutes." "Temples of the devil," they feed their own children with what "belongs to the poor;"[12] instead of growing full on others' salvation at the table of the

[7] Let T 121 to the Signori of Siena.

[8] Let T 204 (DT 5) to Bartolomeo Dominici, O.P.

[9] R 2.4, p. 144.

[10] R 2.4, p. 145.

[11] Let T 357 to King Louis of Hungary.

[12] D 121, p. 233.

cross, they make "taverns their table."[13] They are reduced to "beasts," and "do not so much as know what the Divine Office is,...oh devils and worse than devils."[14]

Church leaders live wedded to luxury and grandeur rather than to the poor, while bishops ordain persons like themselves, "little boys instead of mature men," "idiots who scarcely know how to read and could never pray the Divine Office," ignorant of Latin and unable to say even the words of consecration.[15] Appointed to proclaim God's word "by their life and teaching," these priests shout words that are only "empty sounds."[16] They consider it beneath them to visit the poor; refusing to lift a finger to help, they stand by as others die of hunger. And because they are conscious of their sin, they fear punishment, yet they will not reform their lives; to satisfy their people and to save themselves from further guilt, they merely pretend to say the words of consecration.[17]

So disfigured by sin did the Church appear to Catherine that its very heart, charity, seemed cut out from it.[18] And yet she passionately believed that the way to Christ is through the Church that he loves:[19] "I am the vine, you are the branches; ...apart from me you can do nothing" (Jn 15:5). For Catherine, these words speak no mere metaphor; despite its sin, the Church is still the living body of the Lord through which he continues to pour out the abundance of his saving blood in the sacraments.[20] She begs those cut off from this ecclesial community by interdict or schism to return to the

[13]D 123, p. 235.

[14]D 123, p. 236.

[15]D 129, p. 265.

[16]D 125, p. 240.

[17]D 128, pp. 253-54.

[18]Let T 177 (DT 61) to Cardinal Pietro Corsini of Florence.

[19]Let T 168 (DT 53) to the Elders of Lucca.

[20]Let T 171 (DT 60) to Niccolò Soderini of Florence.

source of their life,[21] to the baptismal bath and Eucharistic meal through which we live.[22]

Catherine grew convinced that if the Church would be reformed its ministry could renew the entire world[23]; yet how could she trust that, despite every human obstacle, the apparently impossible miracle of ecclesial reform would be accomplished? In 1376, Catherine gained in prayer a deepened understanding of the Church's brokenness. Jesus seemed to place the cross on Catherine's shoulder and an olive branch in her hand, inviting her to proclaim to the Church, "I bring you tidings of great joy." This message caused her such gladness that all of her previous sufferings, labor, and prayer seemed as nothing to her. For in the ashes of the Church the Lord showed her the power of his resurrection infusing his own life into the Church's crippled body and restoring its pristine purity as the bride for whom he died.[24]

Even as she saw the Church going "from bad to worse," with its clergy lusting after honor, wealth, and power, the words of the *Exultet* resounded in Catherine's ears: "Oh happy fault that merited such a Redeemer." In the very sin of the Church she recognized the occasion for the priceless gift of reform.[25] As the world's guilt brought down the Savior of the human race to its need, so the Church's sin draws to its poverty this same Redeemer whose power alone can heal and restore it as his poor and humble community.[26] Catherine began to understand that, just as the rose is born only in the midst of thorns,[27] so too the Church's healing and purity are gained only through tribulation.[28]

[21]Let T 168 (DT 53) to the Elders of Lucca.

[22]Let T 207 (DT 68) to the Signori of Florence.

[23]Let T 206 (DT 63) to Pope Gregory XI; Let T 282 to Nicola da Osimo.

[24]Let T 219 (DT 65) to Raymond of Capua and others.

[25]Let T 206 (DT 63) to Pope Gregory XI.

[26]Let T 219 (DT 65) to Raymond of Capua.

[27]Let T 270 to Pope Gregory XI.

[28]Let T 346 to Pope Urban VI.

Proclaim the Word

In the devastation surrounding her, Catherine's own Dominican call inspired her to focus on the fire and zeal of apostolic preaching as a means of Church reform. Raymond writes of more than a thousand people often "crowding in from the mountains and the country districts around Siena just to see her and hear her. And when they heard her or even only had sight of her, their hearts were pierced." So immense was the number of men and women converted by Catherine's words that Raymond alone could not accommodate all who sought the sacrament of reconciliation. He thus sought and obtained Gregory XI's permission for three confessors to accompany her in her preaching missions.[29]

As one of these confessors, Raymond witnessed innumerable times the "mighty flood of heaven's grace" poured out in people's hearts at her words. "I admit that I often sank under the very weight of numbers of the penitents," Raymond confesses; but Catherine, "ever more and more exultant at the booty of souls falling into her victorious hands," seemed to gain increased energy as her labors multiplied, and her gladness on these occasions became nothing less than "contagious."[30]

For inspiration in her preaching, Catherine looked to the apostles, the fiery heralds of God's word who bore Jesus in their hearts and spoke his name like fire on their lips.[31] She reflected on the Spirit's love as it burst into the flaming words the apostles preached at Pentecost. In the Spirit's power, the once timid apostles boldly "mounted the rostrum" of the cross and there tasted Jesus' own hunger for our salvation. Their words thus began to sear the hearts of their hearers like burning "swords prepared in a furnace."[32] And because in their preaching they were not alone—God

[29]R 2.7, p. 227.

[30]*Ibid.*

[31]Let T 51 to Frate Felice da Massa, Augustinian.

[32]Let T 198 (DT 4) to Frate Bartolomeo Dominici, O.P.

was with them—they went to the mouth of death itself without fear. When they did die, it was not from the blows of their persecutors, but from starvation for God's honor and the world's salvation.[33]

Catherine began to understand that she herself and all those who follow in the apostles' footsteps are called to this same zeal; like the clear, pure notes of a trumpet, our preaching is meant to resound through the earth with the joy of God's word:[34] "O infinite goodness! Why doesn't the human heart melt? Why doesn't my heart spill out in my voice?"[35] Yet the passion of her heart *did* spill out in her voice, as Raymond himself witnessed innumerable times. Her "burning words"[36] and the truth she spoke rang with such ardent clarity that the very person of the Spirit seemed to speak through her.[37] To this same kind of zeal Catherine began to urge Raymond himself: "Bear God's word with fire! Pour out the truth, sow the seed of God's word everywhere!"[38]

In her own ministry Catherine drew strength from Dominic, the "fiery bearer of God's word" who consecrated his entire life and energy to preaching the Word. While at prayer, Catherine had once seen Dominic emerge from the Father's breast as radiant bearer of God to the world. She began to urge Dominic's family to claim and to live its charism and to resound as "the voice of Dominic's preaching ...still heard today." For she saw that when their lives begin to preach as radically as their words, when their entire trust is centered not in "polished rhetoric" but in Jesus honored as Lord in their hearts,[39] then will the mouths of his brothers

[33]Let T 280 to Raymond of Capua.

[34]D 121, p. 233.

[35]Pr 15, p. 133.

[36]R 2.8, p. 242.

[37]R 2.10, p. 274.

[38]Let T 280 to Raymond of Capua.

[39]D 125, p. 240.

and sisters be the voice through which Dominic continues to preach and "to be heard."[40]

Catherine was convinced that only the fire of the Spirit taking hold of both preacher and hearer can renew this kind of apostolic preaching. Since the Spirit's power alone renders preaching more than empty words shouted into emptiness,[41] she could not imagine preaching without prayer and intercession on the part of the preacher. Catherine's ardent will and radical trust in the Holy Spirit shaped the boldness of her own intercession: "I will not leave your presence till I see that you have been merciful to them.... It is my will ...and I beg it as a favor that you have mercy on your people."[42]

She learned to implore God's mercy on the world not because we deserve it but because the heart of God will not refuse it: "I beg you to force their wills and dispose them to want what they do not want. I ask this of your infinite mercy."[43] She realizes that God will not refuse the very intercession he inspires: "You cannot resist giving it to whoever asks you for it.... Open, then, unlock and shatter the hardened hearts of your creatures."[44] She asks the Father to give her eyes a fountain of tears to draw his mercy down upon the world, and especially upon his bride, the Church: "O boundless, gentlest charity! This is your garden, implanted in your blood.... Do you, then, be the one to watch over it.... Set our hearts ablaze and plunge them into this blood."[45]

[40]R 2.6, p. 195.

[41]Let T 327 to Frate Andrea of Lucca and others.

[42]D 13, p. 49.

[43]D 134, p. 276.

[44]D 134, p. 275.

[45]Pr 9, p. 71.

The Ministry of Love

As she recognized that the true power of our preaching emanates from how we live, Catherine began to counsel ministers of the Church to suffer with others and to give the service of love with their lives. She writes to Gregory XI that pastors are meant to spend their energies not on material goods but on the infinitely more precious treasure of human persons ransomed by Jesus' blood. Like Jesus himself, they are to lay down, not only their goods for this treasure, but their very lives.[46] And like Paul, they are called to Jesus' own love, encouraging good, becoming weak with the weak, and laboring with zeal for their people's conversion.[47] When their life force begins to be neither selfishness nor fear but only love, they will discover charity not only as their true mother[48] but also as their true wealth, and so will be known as friends of the poor.[49]

From her own experience Catherine knew that we gain this kind of zealous love at no little cost. When her family and friends suffered from the absences required by her ministry, she would remind them of Mary. If there had been no other means for Jesus to ascend the cross, Mary would have offered her own body as the step by which her Son could be crucified. Love great as this filled her only because she had surrendered her entire being to the will and passionate zeal of her Son.[50]

For although the absence of the beloved apostles cost Mary dearly, she loved so generously that after the Resurrection she herself sent them away to preach. Yet neither Mary nor the apostles felt deprived of one another's love; on the contrary, their love grew all the more in absence. Catherine

[46]Let T 209 to Pope Gregory XI.

[47]D 119, p. 228.

[48]Let T 256 to Niccolò, prior of the province of Tuscany.

[49]Let T 341 to Angelo Carraro, first named a bishop and later elected to the papacy, taking the name of Gregory XII. He abdicated after the Council of Florence in 1415 in order to end the schism caused by three papal claimants.

[50]Let T 144 (DT 34) to Monna Pavola at Fiesole.

writes to her friends that she, too, does not abandon them in the travels required by her ministry, but rather loves them all the more deeply "in God."[51]

Catherine found it necessary to encourage even her own mother with these thoughts. Mary loved the apostles "supremely," yet chose to remain alone, as a "guest and pilgrim," deprived of their presence. For their part, the apostles left their mother joyfully, hungry to give their lives for the world's salvation. If they had been asked why they were so joyful in leaving Mary, they would have replied, "Because we have lost ourselves and are enamored of God's honor" and the world's salvation. Catherine gently urges her mother: "I want you to do" the same.[52]

To inspire her own courage and generosity in making the sacrifices entailed by her ministry, Catherine would think also of Paul and Magdalen. Her "little Paul" lived so passionately for others' salvation that he attracted souls as a sponge soaks up water. Bearing the name of Jesus in his heart and on his lips, the "ardent Paul" preached God's word without reserve.[53] "Impassioned for what God loves," he wished to be anathema for his brothers and sisters, if only they would be converted.[54]

Magdalen, too, experienced the love that inflamed the apostles, for she feared no one and refused to give a moment's thought to her own reputation. When the men abandoned him, it was Magdalen who ran to the cross and who stayed with Jesus until his death. And after his death, she also ran to his tomb with the bold and foolish love that would not be kept away from her Lord. She would carry his body herself if she could find where it had been taken. "O Magdalen," Catherine cries out, "you are a fire of love! You do not have your heart, for it was buried with your sweet

---

[51]Let T 118 to Monna Caterina dello Spedaluccio and Giovanna di Capo.

[52]Let T 117 to Monna Lapa and Cecca; Scudder, p. 225.

[53]Let T 226 to Raymond of Capua, O.P.

[54]Let T 204 (DT 5) to Bartolomeo Dominici, O.P.

Lord."[55] It was this passion for the Lord in Mary, in Paul, and in her beloved Magdalen that Catherine began to desire as her own.

Feeding on Souls

As she grew to recognize the face of Jesus in the people she served, Catherine began to ponder his words on the cross, "I thirst" (Jn 19:28). Jesus thirsted for water to moisten his parched lips and throat; but even more, he longed to assuage his ache for our salvation: "It was a great cross for him to carry for such a long time that desire, when he would have liked to see it realized at once."[56] This "cross of desire" tore at him with far more cruelty than the crucifixion which broke open his body. For three hours Jesus suffered excruciating pain on the cross, but he endured an entire lifetime the "infinite torment" of his desire for our healing.[57] Finally, it was not the nails but this very desire which wrested his life from him.[58]

Catherine began to understand that Jesus still cries out to us, "I thirst." Love itself asks us for a drink. Yet our weakness tempts us to feel powerless in slaking Jesus' thirst for our healing. As her own desire to answer the Lord's request grew, Catherine discovered the means we have in our grasp to meet his appeal: we can join our own desire to God's infinite desire. In this way our own zeal can grow intense with the fire of God's love and desire for human healing.[59]

Wood thrown onto a fire becomes itself fire, and the sparks alone are powerful enough to set ablaze an entire city. In this image Catherine found a symbol of what it means to minister for the world's redemption. If we enter through

---

[55]Let T 61 (DT 2) to Monna Agnesa Malavolti and other *mantellate*.

[56]Pr 18, p. 163.

[57]Let T 242 to Angelo da Ricasoli, bishop of Florence.

[58]Let T 136 (DT 37) to Angelo da Ricasoli.

[59]Let T 104 to Raymond of Capua.

prayer and intercession into the furnace of God's mercy, gradually a fire of love so takes hold of us[60] that we cannot help pouring out our life for our brothers and sisters.[61]

"I have earnestly desired to eat this passover with you before I suffer" (Lk 22:15). Our desire for something can be so intense that the desire itself causes us pain. Catherine recognized the suffering which devoured Jesus as the pain of his longing to die for us and yet of his having to wait for its accomplishment. She pictures Jesus not shrinking from the cross but running toward it, wild with love;[62] as a choking person gasps for air, Jesus grasped the means of slaking the thirst for our redemption which for so long had tormented him.

In a spirited discussion with Raymond, Catherine once argued that the prayer of Jesus, "Remove this cup from me" (Lk 22:42), evokes far different interpretations from "heroic" persons than from those who shrink from death. Fearful people interpret this passage as expressing Jesus' desire to escape death, but those full of zealous love see in it his eagerness for death. The "cup" was his desire for the world's salvation, a cup from which "he had been drinking all his life long...and which now, as the great hour drew near, he was drinking with greater eagerness than ever." His plea, "Remove this cup from me," thus voiced his impatient desire to drink the cup of his passion to the last drop in one great final draught of love.[63]

"I have earnestly desired to eat this passover with you before I suffer" (Lk 22:15). Catherine realized that the God who needs no physical food acts toward us like one starved, delighting in our healing as if it were the richest of foods. And precisely because he longs to share with us this "pasch

[60]Let T 228 to Neri di Landoccio.

[61]Let T 183 (DT 56) to Iacopo da Itri, bishop of Otrante, who chose allegiance to Clement VII and was rewarded for his loyalty by being named cardinal legate to the Queen of Naples. Through political intrigue, however, he was imprisoned and died in the most wretched of circumstances.

[62]Let T 78 to Niccolò Povero, hermit at Florence.

[63]R 2.6, p. 198.

of desire," he asks us to starve for the food of souls and to "eat" them through our prayer and ministry. The zeal that filled Jesus began to feed and invigorate Catherine herself more deeply than physical food could nourish her. Like a person starving, she learned to "devour souls," for she discovered that the healing of our brothers and sisters becomes a food that marvelously fills us. Pushed out of its narrow limitations, our heart's capacity to love expands until it is able to embrace the entire world.

But with Paul, Catherine also found that feeding on others' salvation requires a high price: hardship and sleepless nights, ministering and preaching often without apparent reward.[64] We find, then, that the cross itself becomes the table where we eat and devour souls. Catherine pictures her beloved Dominic inviting his family to "do nothing else but stand at this table by the light of learning," and to seek only God's glory and the world's redemption.[65] As we increasingly eat at this table, we will find God accomplishing far greater marvels than our limited efforts could produce,[66] for the Holy Spirit will achieve in and through us outcomes that are impossible to us alone.[67]

A Life Poured Out for the Church

Catherine desperately wanted to see realized the ecclesiastical reform for which she labored; but, as the prospect of its achievement grew more and more dim, the weight of the tragedy began to crush her body and spirit. She writes to a friend that giving her own life a thousand times a day for the Church would still seem to her only a drop in the ocean,[68] for she increasingly believed herself responsible for the con-

---

[64]Let T 296 to Don Giovanni of the Cells.

[65]D 158, p. 338.

[66]Let T 55 to Don William, prior general of the Carthusains.

[67]Let T 105 (DT 8) to Frate Bartolomeo Dominici, O.P.

[68]Let T 282 to Nicola da Osimo.

tradition between the purity the Church should have and the sin that in fact poisoned it. If only her prayer and labor were more faithful, the Church surely would be reformed.[69]

Yet in Catherine's eyes, her own efforts seemed to hinder this reform: "My life is of very little use to anyone else; rather is it painful and oppressive to every person far and near, by reason of my sins."[70] It was her "many sins" that had prevented the Church's renewal[71] and caused persecution of the pope: "If he [Urban VI] complains of me he is right."[72] Desire for the Church's reform now began to consume Catherine in a pain which caused her to die and yet prevented her from dying.[73] She had already spent her every energy for the "sweet bride of Christ" and now had nothing left to give but the "marrow of her bones."[74] Unable to shed her blood for the Church in death, she would make of her remaining days a living martyrdom: "I have one body, and to you I offer and return it." The vehemence of Catherine's passion to die for the Church emboldened her to take Jesus' words as her own: "Here is my flesh; here is my blood.... Let my bones be split apart for those for whom I am praying.... Let my...marrow be ground up for your vicar on earth, your bride's only spouse."[75]

"Christ loved the Church and gave himself up for her that he might present the Church to himself in splendor, without spot or wrinkle" (Eph 5:25-26). It was not for a holy and spotless Church that Catherine felt called to give her life, but like Jesus, for a people wounded and corrupt. For this damaged "bride of Christ" no effort seemed enough: we are called to love and serve the Church not simply in good times but also and especially in her hour of need. After the aborted

[69]Let T 214 to Catarina dello Spedaluccio and Giovanna di Capo.

[70]Let T 119 to Monna Alessa; Scudder, p. 232.

[71]Let T 214 to Catarina della Spedaluccio and Giovanna di Capo.

[72]Let T 267 to Raymond of Capua; Scudder, p. 239.

[73]Let T 211 (DT 70) to Raymond of Capua.

[74]Let T 267 to Raymond of Capua; Scudder, p. 241.

[75]Pr 1, p. 20.

attempt on her life at Florence, Catherine had written to
Raymond of her bitter disappointment that her blood had
been unworthy to reconcile the Church. "How happy my
soul would have been had I given my blood" for the "sweet
spouse, the Church."[76] And to the Queen of Hungary she
had written: "I. . .have nothing to help her with. If my blood
would be of any use, I would open up my body and shed it
all."[77]

Because love had given her eyes to see past the Church's
sin into its very heart, Catherine increasingly viewed the
Church as the home of all good, the place where Jesus
washes us clean and feeds us with his own body.[78] The more
she felt the contradiction between what the Church is and
what it should be, therefore, the more she strained to overcome this contradiction in her own body. Toward the end of
Gregory's papacy she writes to Raymond of a mystical experience in which God asks her to offer herself anew for this
wounded bride—an invitation which so deeply affected her
that she made it the basis for her book, the *Dialogue.* In
prayer Catherine seemed to gaze at the entire universe held
lovingly in the hands of God. "All are mine," the Father told
her, and "no one can be taken from me. . . . And because
they came forth from me, I love them ineffably and will
show them mercy by means of my servants."[79]

Catherine saw further that Christ, the "door" of the
Church, opens us to the very abyss of the Trinity. So radiant
did the Church appear to her that she began to long for
everyone to know and possess its treasure. It was then that
she felt the Lord asking her to give herself anew for his
broken community. "To this work I have appointed you—
you and all who follow you or are to follow,. . .devote, then,
your life and heart and mind wholly to that Bride for me,
with no regard for yourself." At an earlier age, Catherine

[76]Let T 295 to Raymond of Capua.

[77]Let T 145 (DT 40) to the Queen Mother of Hungary; Noffke, trans.

[78]Let T 207 (DT 68) to the Signori of Florence.

[79]Let T 371 to Raymond of Capua; Scudder, p. 345.

had hesitated when the Lord drew her from solitude into the midst of her brothers and sisters. There was no hesitation now: "I have nothing to give except what you have given me. Take then my heart."[80]

For some time, Catherine had felt the pain of Raymond's absence from Rome in her trial. Yet although he would have been the "very greatest consolation" to her, she writes to him of her even greater "consolation and gladness" at his labors on behalf of the Church. In this same letter—the last we have from her—Catherine confides to Raymond her own experience of a living martyrdom for the Church. On Sexagesima Sunday of 1380, as she fell under the weight of the pain and paralysis that would last until her death in April of that same year, Catherine felt the Lord promise to continue remaking the vessel of her body in and for the Church. The sacrifice of her prayer and tears and tormenting desire would replace the physical labors she could no longer undertake for the Lord's community. "My life is consumed and shed for this sweet Bride: I by this road, and the glorious martyrs with blood."[81]

God had invited Catherine when she was young to a mission whose path would lead her beyond her cell and city to the Church and world. But her vocation to labor in and for the Church had deprived her of heaven when she had so longed for death. Precisely because they had cost her so much, love for her brothers and sisters flamed into the enduring passion of her life until her prayer and suffering became a living intercession for them.[82] And gradually, in light of this love, she began to see hell itself in a different way. "I could wish that I myself were accursed and cut off from Christ" for the sake of others' salvation (Rom 9:3). Provided that she could still love God, she would gladly endure forever hell's torments if all others could be saved. Even more, she would make of her own body a stopper

---

[80]*Ibid.*

[81]Let T 373 to Raymond of Capua; Scudder, pp. 348-49.

[82]R 2.6, p. 205.

against hell, setting herself upon the very mouth of hell to close it, and to "prevent any further souls from entering it." The force of her love grew so passionate that she longed even to annihilate hell: "I would love that hell should be wiped out; or at least that no soul should ever go there again."[83]

As Catherine's body grew more weak and broken with time, it seemed increasingly unable to contain the fire that inflamed her spirit. Earlier in her life, she had undergone a mystical "death" as this same fire within her seemed to break her heart in two.[84] Only later would Raymond see how clearly this experience would foreshadow her physical death. In the *Dialogue* Catherine had described the life and death of those yielded to God in precisely the way she herself had been: "Their hearts were vessels of affection that carried" God's name to the world and "proclaimed it with burning love." At death, their hearts break open "with unspeakable love" and with one last overwhelming impulse of love "seize" the prize.[85] Much later, Raymond would look with new eyes at these words describing men and women consumed by God's love, and see in them a portrait of Catherine's own death: "Not for any natural cause, or for any other reason than the sheer intensity of her love for God, she breathed her last."[86]

At her death, the immense mystical fire within Catherine broke through to its goal. The passionate heart which had spent itself for the Church finally came home to the heart of the triune God who had claimed her entire being. As she promised, she lives now with Jesus to make intercession for us (Heb 7:25). May her tenderness and ardor continue to draw those who seek the living God as surely as it drew the disciples of her day. And may the zeal for God's house which consumed her inflame us with a passion that will set fire to the world she so loved.

---

[83]R Prologue, p. 14.

[84]R 2.6, p. 202-03.

[85]D 131, p. 265.

[86]R 2.6, p. 201.

APPENDIX I
AN OUTLINE CHRONOLOGY
OF CATHERINE'S LIFE

1347	Catherine is born in Siena on March 25.
1348	Siena suffers its first bout with the Plague.
c. 1354	Catherine consecrates herself to God.
1362	Bonaventura, Catherine's sister and confidante, dies.
	At the advice of Tommaso dalla Fonte, O.P., her first confessor and director, she cuts off her hair as a way to offset marriage plans.
c. 1365	At about the age of eighteen, she receives the Dominican habit of the *mantellate* and begins a three-year period of solitude during which she also learns to read.
1368	Jesus espouses her mystically to himself, calling her out of solitude to serve Siena's poor and sick.
	On August 22, Catherine's father dies.
	Bartolomeo Dominici, O.P. becomes her second confessor.
1370	Catherine undergoes a "mystical death" which opens her to a more extensive ministry in an ever widening circle of influence.
1374	At the age of twenty-seven, Catherine undertakes her first trip to Florence and acquires

Raymond of Capua, O.P. as her confessor and director.

She ministers to Plague victims in Siena.

1375   Catherine journeys to Pisa in an attempt to dissuade Pisa and Lucca from joining the anti-papal league.

Here she spends the major portion of the year and gains new vigor in preaching a crusade to the Holy Land.

In Pisa she experiences light from Jesus' wounds transfixing her with invisible stigmata.

In the summer she ministers to Niccolò di Tuldo at his execution in Siena.

1376   Catherine volunteers her aid in mediating with Pope Gregory XI for the release of Florence from interdict.

She travels to Avignon to meet with the pope on Florence's behalf.

Her energies focus on Church reform, preaching the crusade, and encouraging Gregory's fidelity to his promise of returning the papal residence to Rome.

On September 13, Gregory sets out for Rome.

1377   Gregory solemnly enters Rome on January 13.

Catherine founds a monastery of nuns in the fortress at Belcaro donated by Nanni di Ser Vanni.

From May until December, Catherine stays at the Salimbeni castle in Rocca d'Orcia in order to mediate peace between feuding family members.

Raymond leaves Siena to assume his responsibilities as prior of the Church of the Minerva in Rome.

Catherine perhaps learns to write, and a mystical experience at Rocca d'Orcia leads her to begin her "Book," the *Dialogue*.

In December, she returns home to Siena.

1378   In early 1378 or late 1377, Catherine travels to Florence at the invitation of Gregory XI in order to mediate peace between him and the Florentines.

In Florence she continues composing her book through dictation to her secretaries.

Gregory XI dies on March 27, and on April 8 Bartolomeo Prignano is elected as Urban VI.

On June 18, to her sorrow, Catherine escapes assassination as a suspected accomplice of the Guelphs.

In late July or early August, the papacy achieves peace with Florence.

Catherine travels to Siena and completes her *Dialogue* in October.

Schismatic cardinals gather at Fondi and on September 20 elect Cardinal Count Robert of Geneva as rival pope Clement VII.

On November 28, Catherine arrives in Rome, at Urban's request, to support him in the papal schism.

Urban sends Raymond on a papal mission to France in early December.

1379   Living with a large number of her disciples in Rome, Catherine gives her energies to the work of Church unity and reform.

The majority of her recorded prayers stem from this time.

Her health declines.

1380   Against the backdrop of Roman uprisings and deepening schism, Catherine becomes increasingly ill.

Unable to eat or drink beginning January 1, she continues to make the mile-long journey daily to St. Peter's, where she spends each day interceding for Church reform and unity.

On February 26, she becomes paralyzed.

Catherine dies on April 29.

APPENDIX II
SIGNIFICANT TEXTS, EDITIONS, AND
TRANSLATIONS OF CATHERINE'S WRITINGS

Two groups of writings comprise the sources from which we learn about Catherine: a) her own writings—382 extant letters, the *Dialogue*, and 26 extant prayers collected by her disciples as she prayed aloud; b) the testimony of those who knew her. This latter body of material includes the following:

1. Her confessor Raymond of Capua's biography of Catherine, the *Legenda Major* (written between 1384-95).

2. Two writings of her Dominican disciple Tommaso d'Antonio Nacci da Siena (called "Caffarini"):

    a. the *Libellus de Supplemento*, an expansion of Raymond's biography, employing the notes of her first confessor, Tommaso dalla Fonte;

    b. the *Legenda Minor*, Caffarini's abridged version of the *Libellus*.

3. The *Processus* of Venice, the testimony of Catherine's disciples which Caffarini started to compile in 1411 for her canonization process.

4. *Letters* of her disciples to Catherine and to one another, including Barduccio Canigiani's account of her death to Suor Caterina Petriboni.

5. The *Miracoli* by an unknown Florentine.

6. The *Memoirs* of her disciple Cristofano di Gano.

7. Some short writings of the English Augustinian friar William Flete.

8. Poems in her honor by her disciples.

None of Catherine's writings exist in her own hand. We indicate here only the most significant manuscripts and printed editions, as well as English translations of her works.

The Letters

1. *Manuscripts*

a. Palatino 3514, Biblioteca Nazionale, Florence; traceable to her secretary, Neri di Landoccio Pagliaresi.

b. Magliabechiano XXXVIII, 130, Biblioteca Nazionale, Florence; traceable to Pagliaresi.

c. Magliabechiano XXXV, 199, Biblioteca Nazionale, Florence; traceable to Pagliaresi.

d. Ms. AD.XIII.34, Biblioteca Braidense, Milan; traceable to her secretary Stefano di Corrado Maconi.

e. Palatino 57, Biblioteca Nazionale, Florence; traceable to Maconi.

f. Ms. 292, Biblioteca Casanatense, Rome; traceable to her secretary Barduccio Canigiani.

2. *Printed Editions*

a. Aldo Manuzio: Venice, 1500, 1548, 1562, 1564.

b. Girolamo Gigli: Siena and Lucca, 1713.

c. Niccolò Tommasèo: Berbera-Florence, 1860.

d. Piero Misciatelli, a republishing of the Tommasèo edition: Siena, 1912-22.

3. *Critical Edition*

Eugenio Dupré Theseider began a critical edition of Catherine's letters and published the first volume containing eighty-eight letters in Rome, 1940; this work is currently being pursued by Antonio Volpata.

4. *English Translations*

a. V. D. Scudder, trans. and ed. *Selected letters of Catherine Benincasa: Saint Catherine of Siena as Seen in Her Letters.* New York: E. P. Dutton and Co., 1927.

b. Kenelm Foster, O.P., and Mary John Ronayne, O.P.,

trans. and eds. *I, Catherine: Selected Writings of Catherine of Siena.* London: Collins, 1980.

c. Suzanne Noffke, O.P., is general editor of a projected 4 volume English translation of the entirety of Catherine's 382 extant letters. The work is based on the Italian critical edition begun by Dupré Theseider and presently being pursued by Antonio Volpato in Rome, under the auspices of the *Istituto storico italiano per il medio evo.* Volume one, containing an English translation of Dupré Theseider's critical edition of 88 of Catherine's letters, is now ready for publication.

The Dialogue

1. *Manuscripts*

a. Ms. 292, Biblioteca Casanatense, Rome; traceable to Barduccio Canigiani.

b. Ms. T.II.9, BViblioteca Communale, Siena; traceable to Stefano Maconi.

c. Ms. T.6.5, Biblioteca Estense, Modena.

2. *Printed Editions*

a. Baldassare Azzuguidi: Bologna, 1472.

b. Printed editions in Naples, Venice, and Brescia in the fifteenth century; Ferrara and Venice, sixteenth century; Venice, seventeenth century.

c. Girolamo Gigli: Siena, 1707.

d. Matilde Fiorilli: Bari, 1912.

e. Innocenzo Taurisano: Florence, 1928.

f. D. Umberto Meattini: Rome, 1969.

g. Guiliana Cavallini: Rome, 1968; reprint, 1980.

3. *Critical Edition*

Although no critical edition exists, the work of Guiliana Cavallini comes closest to the task.

4. *English Translations*

a. Dane James, ed. *The Orcherde of Syon.* London: Wynkyn de Worde, 1519. This work translates a Latin translation by an unknown author for the nuns of the monastery of Syon, England, in the fifteenth century.

b. Phyllis Hodgson and Gabriel M. Liegey, eds. *The Orchard of Syon*, vol I: Text. The Early English Text Society, vol. 258. London: Oxford U. Press, 1966.

c. Algar Thorold, trans. *The Dialogue of the Seraphic Virgin Catherine of Siena.* London: Kegan, Paul, Trench, Tuber, 1896. This edition lacked only chapters 135-53 on divine providence; later editions omitted far more sections.

d. Suzanne Noffke, O.P., trans. *Catherine of Siena: The Dialogue.* New York: Paulist Press, 1980. This work, based on Cavallini's Italian edition, translates the whole of the *Dialogue* into English.

Prayers

1. *Manuscripts*
   a. Ms. XIV.24, Archives of the General Curia of the Order of Preachers, Rome.

   b. Ms. T.II.7, Biblioteca Communale degl'Intronati, Siena.

   c. Ms. I.VI.14, Biblioteca Communale degl'Intronati, Siena.

   d. Palatino 3154, Biblioteca Nazionale, Vienna.

2. *Printed Editions*
   a. Aldo Manuzio: Venice, 1500.
   b. Girolamo Gigli: Siena, 1707.
   c. Innocenzo Taurisano: Rome, 1920.

3. *Critical Edition*
   Guiliana Cavallini: Rome, 1978.

4. *English Translation*
   Suzanne Noffke, O.P., trans. and ed. *The Prayers of Catherine of Siena.* New York: Paulist Press, 1983.

Selected Bibliography

SOURCES

Anonimo Fiorentino. *I miracoli di Caterina di Iacopo da Siena.* Ed. Francesco Valli. Vol. 4 of *Fontes Vitae S. Catharinae Senensis Historici.* Ed. M. H. Laurent. Siena: R. Universita di Siena Cattedra Cateriniana, 1936.

Canigiani, Barduccio. *Il transito di Santa Caterina.* In *Lettere di S. Caterina da Siena, ridotte a miglior lezione, e in ordine nuovo disposte con note di Niccolò Tommasèo.* Ed. Piero Misciatelli. 6 vols. Siena: Giuntini & Bentivoglio, 1913-1922. 6: 148-153.

Catherine of Siena. *The Dialogue.* Trans. Suzanne Noffke, O.P. New York: Paulist Press, 1980.

_____. *Epistolario di Santa Caterina da Siena.* Ed. Eugenio Dupré Theseider. In *Fonti per la storia d'Italia, pubblicate dal R. Istituto storico italiano per il medio evo.* Roma: nella sede dell'Istituto, 1940. One of 4 projected volumes; work currently being pursued by Antonio Volpato.

_____. *I, Catherine: Selected Writings of Catherine of Siena.* Trans. Kenelm Foster, O.P. and Mary John Ronayne, O.P. London: Collins, 1980.

_____. *Lettere di S. Caterina da Siena, ridotte a miglio lezione, e in ordine nuovo disposte con note di Niccolò Tommaseò.* Ed. Piero Misciatelli. 6 vols. Siena: Giuntini & Bentivoglio, 1913-1922.

_____. *The Prayers of Catherine of Siena.* Trans. Suzanne Noffke, O.P. New York: Paulist Press, 1983.

_____. *Selected Letters of Catherine Benincasa: Saint Catherine of Siena as Seen in her Letters.* Trans. Vida Scudder. London: J. M. Dent & Sons, Ltd., and New York: E.P. Dutton, 1927.

Cristofano di Gano Guidini. *Memorie di ser Cristofano.* Ed. Innocenzo Taurisano. *In Fioretti di Santa Caterina da Siena.* 2nd ed. Roma: Ferrari, 1927. 111-134.

Grottanelli, Francesco. *Leggenda minore di S. Caterina da Siena e Lettere dei suoi discepoli.* Bologna: Gaetano Romagnoli, 1868.

Laurent, Marie-Hyacinthe, ed. *Leggenda abbreviata di S. Caterina da Siena di F. Antonio della Rocca.* Vol. 15 of *Fontes vitae S. Catharinae Senensis historici.* Firenze: Sansoni; and Siena: Stab. tip. S. Bernardino, 1939.

_____, ed. and Francesco Valli, ed. *I miracoli de S. Caterina da Siena.* Vol. 4 of *Fontes vitae S. Catharinae Senensis historici.* Firenze: Sansoni, 1936..

_____, ed. *Il Processo Castellano.* Vol. IX of *Fontes vitae S. Catharinae Senensis historici.* Milano: Bocca, 1942.

Raymond of Capua. *Legenda major.* Trans. Giuseppe Tinagli. Siena: Cantagalli, 1934.

_____. *The Life of Catherine of Siena.* Trans. Conleth Kearns, O.P. Wilmington, Del.: Michael Glazier, Inc., 1980.

Tommaso di Antonio da Siena (Caffarini). *Leggenda minore di S. Caterina da Siena e lettere dei suoi discepoli.* Ed. Francesco Grottanelli. Bologna: n.p., 1868.

_____. *Libellus de Supplemento: Legende prolixe Virginis Beate Catherine de Senis.* Ed., Giuliana Cavallini, Imelda Foralosso. Roma: Edizioni Cateriniane, 1974.

STUDIES AND BIOGRAPHIES

Ashley, O.P., Benedict. "Guide to Saint Catherine's Dialogue," *Cross and Crown* 29 (1977): 237-249.

_____. "St. Catherine of Siena's Principles of Spiritual Direction," *Spirituality Today* 33 (1981): 43-52.

Connor, O.P., Paul. "Catherine of Siena and Raymond of Capua: A Friendship in Perspective," *Review for Religious* 40 (1981): 32-39.

Curtayne, Alice. *Saint Catherine of Siena.* London: Sheed and Ward, 1932.

Drane, Augusta Theodosia. *The History of St. Catherine of Siena and Her Companions.* 4th ed. 2 vols. London: Longmans, Green and Col, 1915.

Finnegan, O.P., Jeremy. "St. Catherine in England: The Orchard of Syon," *Spirituality Today* 32 (1980): 13-24.

Flood, O.P., Marie Walter. "St. Thomas's Thought in the *Dialogue* of St. Catherine," *Spirituality Today* 32 (1980): 25-35.

Foster, O.P., Kenelm. "St. Catherine's Teaching on Christ," *Life of the Spirit* 16 (1962): 310-323.

Gardner, Edmund G. *Saint Catherine of Siena: A Study in the Religion, Literature and History of the Fourteenth Century In Italy.* London: Dent; New York: Dutton & Co., 1907.

Giordani, Igino. *Saint Catherine of Siena.* Trans. Thomas J. Tobin. Boston: St. Paul Editions, 1975.

Jorgensen, Johannes. *Saint Catherine of Siena.* Trans. Ingeborg Lund. London and New York: Longmans, Green, and Co., 1939.

Levasti, Arrigo. *My Servant, Catherine*. Trans. Dorothy White. Westminster, Md.: Newman Press, 1954.

Noffke, O.P., Suzanne. "Catherine of Siena: Mission and Ministry in the Church," *Review for Religious* 39 (1980): 183-195.

_____."Demythologizing Catherine: The Wealth of Internal Evidence," *Spirituality Today* 32 (1980): 4-11.

O' Driscoll, O.P., Mary. "Mercy for the World: St. Catherine's View of Intercessory Prayer," *Spirituality Today* 32 (1980): 36-45.

Parks, O.P., Carola. "Social and Political Consciousness in the letters of Catherine of Siena," *Listening* 13 (1978): 258-267.

Perrin, Joseph Marie. *Catherine of Siena*. Trans. Paul Barrett. Westminster, Md.: Newman Press, 1965.

Reges, O.P., Marie Stephen. "Reflections on St. Catherine as Daughter of Divine Wisdom," *Spirituality Today* 32 (1980): 46-56.

Schneiders, I.H.M., Sandra. "Spiritual Discernment in the Dialogue of Saint Catherine of Siena," *Horizons* 9 (1982): 47-59.

Weber, O.P., Richard K. "The Historical Quality of St. Albert's and St. Catherine's Sanctity," *Spirituality Today* 32 (1980): 325-335.

Name Index

Subject Index